THE GIRLS' GUIDE
TO
POWER & SUCCESS

SUSAN WILSON SOLOVIC

MJF BOOKS
NEW YORK

Published by MJF Books
Fine Communications
322 Eighth Avenue
New York, NY 10001

The Girl's Guide to Power and Success
LC Control Number 2002093839
ISBN 1-56731-563-1

This edition published by arrangement with AMACOM, a division of American Management Association.

Manufactured in the United States of America on acid-free paper ∞

MJF Books and the MJF colophon are trademarks of Fine Creative Media, Inc.

QM   10 9   8   7   6   5   4

This book is dedicated to my parents,

Ray and Lucille Wilson,

and to my husband, George Solovic—

you gave me the courage to succeed.

CONTENTS

Introduction   xi

O N E : The Power of Expectations   **1**

Pretty Good for a Girl   **1**

Two Hundred Years and We Haven't Arrived   **4**

Same Job—Different Pay   **7**

Reach for the Moon   **10**

T W O : The Power of a "Go for It" Attitude   **11**

Don't Wait for Permission   **11**

Don't Wait for an Invitation   **13**

Build a Supportive Team   **14**

Find a Role Model   **16**

Look for Companies That "Get It"   **18**

Play to Your Audience   **21**

T H R E E : The Power of 20/20 Vision   **24**

You Can't Fight It If You Don't See It   **24**

You Can't Escape It—Discrimination Is Everywhere   **28**

Watch out for Men Who Still Don't "Get It"   **32**

Empower Yourself—Know Your Rights   **35**

Be Part of the Solution, Not the Problem   **39**

F O U R : The Power of Communicating Like a Pro   **42**

It's Not about What You Say—It's How You Say It   **42**

Speak the Same Language   **46**

The Saga of the Invisible Woman   47

Intimacy Doesn't Work in the Boardroom   50

Don't Dish the Dirt with the Guys   51

Watch out for the "But" Syndrome   52

Don't Wait for Your Turn—Interrupt   53

Drill Down to the Bottom Line   55

Why Don't You Say What You Really Mean?   57

Break the Mold   60

Giggling Is for Little Girls   61

Stop Saying That You're Sorry   62

FIVE: The Power of Pizzazz: Creating Personal Charisma   65

What Is Charisma?   65

Create a Signature Look   67

Be the Boss of Your Body   69

Create a Special Connection   72

Put on a Happy Face   73

Don't Put Yourself Down   75

Learn to Take Compliments Graciously   76

If You Can't Say Something Nice, Don't
    Say Anything at All   77

Mind Your Ps & Qs   78

Never "Wing It"   79

SIX: The Power of a Blended Leadership Style   81

A New Economy—New Opportunities   81

It's Okay to Use a Little Feminine Charm   84

You Need a Little Chutzpah   86

There Are Some People You Just Can't Save   88

Avoid Being Sabotaged by an Open Door   90

Don't Take It Personally   92

Don't Shy away from Confrontation   93

Frazzled Isn't a Good Look—Keep Your
    Emotions in Check   **96**
You Can Negotiate Anything   **98**

SEVEN: The Power of Planning   **102**
Taking It One Step at a Time   **102**
Wow Them   **104**
Taking Risk Is Part of the Game—Go for It   **107**
Power Comes from a Positive Attitude   **110**
Moving Onward and Upward   **111**
Be Open to Lateral or Interindustry Moves   **113**

EIGHT: The Power of a Turbocharged Career   **117**
Mentors Can Turbocharge Your Success   **117**
How to Find a Mentor   **118**
Ask for What You Want   **120**
Hire a Professional Coach   **122**
Watch out for the Threatened Woman   **124**
Technology—The Gender Equalizer   **127**
Education—Your Most Prized Possession   **131**
Read Everything You Can Get Your Hands On   **133**
Break through the Mundane—Color
    outside the Lines   **135**
Successful Women Thrive on Competition   **137**
Become a Networking Queen   **139**
Be Inclusive, Not Exclusive   **142**

NINE: The Power of Balance   **145**
Be a Superstar, Not a Superwoman   **145**
"I Can Handle It!"   **146**
Hire a Cleaning Lady   **149**
Go with Your Gut   **150**
Follow Your Passion   **151**

Defining Success Creates Personal Power   153
The Power of Pampering   155
Learn to Say No, and Mean It   159
Become a Good Time Manager   160

TEN: **The Power of Advocacy**   163
Recapture the Spirit of a Day Gone By   163
The Underrepresented Majority   164
We Need a Woman's Voice   167
Finding Your Role in the Process   168
Get out Your Checkbook   170
Building a Bridge   172

ELEVEN: **The Power of Money**   174
Women Start off from a Weak Position   178
Show Me the Money   180
Money Means Power and Freedom   183
No Excuses—Do It   184
Be Selfish—Pay Yourself First   186

TWELVE: **A Vision for the Future**   189
A Feminine World   189
Men and Women Want the Same Things   191
Our Duty as Role Models for the Next Generation   193
Successful Women Speak about the Future   197

M any people have asked why I wanted to write a success book for women when there are already so many on the market. The simple answer is that I am passionate about helping women to succeed. I have personally either experienced or witnessed much discrimination in my life, and I am tired of it. I am fed up with being a victim of societal prejudice, bias, and stereotyping. I am intolerant of people who think that I am a secretary or a housewife simply because I am a woman. I am angered when people assume that my husband is the primary breadwinner in our family. My name is not "sweetie" or "honey" to anyone other than members of my family, and I am not interested in exchanging recipes over lunch.

So a few summers ago, while recovering from back surgery, I began to put my thoughts on paper. Effortlessly, I filled pages with my own personal stories and experiences. Then, I began interviewing successful women from all across the country. I talked to young women, older women, women entrepreneurs, women executives, women from different industries and women in politics. Interestingly enough, I heard similar stories from all of these women, regardless of their background or level of achievement.

Originally, my idea was to share the insight that I gathered from these successful women, along with my own advice, to help other women avoid pitfalls and obstacles in their personal journeys toward success. However, as I began the writing process, I realized women continue to fight the same battles over and over again because we do not understand the concept of power and how to leverage it.

Success alone is not enough. It is one piece of the puzzle, and a very important one. But success without power is nothing. Power originates from having a voice and being able to effectuate change. Historically, women's voices have had little, if no impact. Imagine about how different the world would be if our voices were heard.

Although some women have broken through the "glass ceiling," many who have are viewed as tokens. Unfortunately, they are the exception, not the rule. That is why there is a media frenzy whenever a woman is named chief executive officer of a major corporation or steps out as a viable presidential candidate. The focus is not on her experience or ability to lead, but on her gender, because that is the "real" story.

For women to gain power as a gender, they need critical mass. *The Girls' Guide to Power and Success* teaches women how to obtain gender parity and how to combine success and power, both personally and collectively. It outlines how a woman can be in charge of her life and have the ability to create her own success on her own terms.

The word *power*, in and of itself, can have pejorative connotations. But the power described in this book is a multidimensional positive force. On a personal level, power is the ability to produce the results that we desire most. This ability begins by overcoming the mental barriers that impede success and raising personal expectations. Nearly all of us suffer from the "good girl" syndrome, which limits our ability to compete effectively in the business world.

Power is also about granting yourself permission to be successful—to follow your passions and live out your dreams. You must turn off negative messages that dictate what you "should" do, instead of what you want to do. Power comes from fearlessly taking risks and striving for excellence. Power hinges on economic freedom and broad personal networks. Finally, an essential element of power for women centers on our ability to work together to leverage our collective voices so that we can be the leaders of change and leave a legacy of equality for future generations.

It is time to challenge yourself to take control of and responsibility for your personal destiny. We all do many things, either consciously or unconsciously, to sabotage our success, which allows the cycle of subordination and prejudice to continue. Your first step toward power and success is to stop thinking like a good girl, and to begin acting like a smart, savvy woman. The experience and expertise shared in the pages of this book should serve as a guide for you, but ultimately the task is yours.

THE GIRLS' GUIDE
TO
POWER & SUCCESS

THE POWER OF EXPECTATIONS

"Whether you think you can or whether you think you can't, you're right."

—Henry Ford

Pretty Good for a Girl

Since the late 1800s, women have experienced sweeping and dramatic changes in their lives. One can only imagine what life must have been like for our great-grandmothers at the beginning of the twentieth century. Women could not vote. They were likely to die in childbirth. Educational opportunities were limited, and women were barred from most professions. As a general rule, women could not testify in court, and they could not serve on juries. Married women had only recently won the right to own property in their own name. Women were second-class citizens.

As the old saying goes, "You've come a long way baby." Or have we? Although significant strides have been made toward equality for women, real progress continues to plod along at a snail's pace. Societal attitudes toward women are deeply rooted in our history and significantly impede our efforts to make a mark in the business world. At best, there exists an attitude of ambivalence toward women in the workplace. However, there is another attitude looming dangerously in the shadows of the American mind-set that a woman's place is in the home.

A number of years ago, I was recruited by a large privately held company for the position of vice president/director of marketing. After breezing through the preliminary interviews with an all-male cadre of key executives, I was asked to meet with the chief executive officer (CEO). On the day of the scheduled interview, I was escorted into a large, extravagantly decorated office where the silver-haired, distinguished-looking CEO sat at the head of a long mahogany conference table. He stood and greeted me, and we exchanged the obligatory pleasantries. Then, he began asking standard questions about my work experience and accomplishments. After a few minutes, he stopped almost midsentence and peered at me over the top of his half-frame reading glasses. "You've done very well for a woman. I bet you never thought you'd do so well," he said.

Unbelievable! My mouth dropped open, and I wondered what decade this man was living in. My first reaction was to stand up, make a stinging James Carville–like rebuttal, turn on my heels, and storm out, slamming the door behind me. But I did not. I just sat there. Without showing any indication of my indignation, I politely smiled and pathetically mumbled something about how fortunate I had been in my career. Amazingly, I survived the remainder of the interview, charmingly thanked him for his time, and exited the office building. Once outside, I literally sprinted to my car. Frantically, I unlocked the door and slid inside. Safely ensconced in the solitude of my car, I took a deep breath, leaned my head back, and shut my eyes. My heart pounded and my mind raced. "What a jerk," I thought to myself. "I wouldn't work for that guy if it were the last job on earth."

On my drive home from the interview, the scene played over and over in my mind. The magnitude of his words and my meek reaction troubled and perplexed me, until a realization finally hit me. I was angry because in an ironic, almost obtuse way, the CEO's remarks were a backhanded compliment. Admittedly, it was not a politically correct thing for him to say, but I realized that he had expressed what a lot of men (and women) think when they see a successful woman. Because there are relatively few high-ranking, successful women, we are seen as anomalies—a novelty.

Furthermore, much to my chagrin, a certain part of me agreed with him: I had done "pretty good for a girl." In comparison with my female friends and colleagues, I led the pack and set the standards. As the first woman executive in a male-dominated, international asset-based lending company, I had cracked the glass ceiling. Compared with other women, I made a lot of money. However, although I made a six-figure income, my salary fell approximately $20,000 short of my male predecessors'. There were other differences, too. When I was promoted into the position, the company's policy on corporate cars conveniently changed, making my position no longer eligible. Then there were the fancy company trips to Europe and Hawaii, which the men who had proceeded me always attended, but somehow my name never found its way on an invitation list. Feeling powerless, I naively ignored the unequal treatment and never complained because I did not expect more.

That lack of expectation brings me to the critical question that we must all ask ourselves: Why do we differentiate between what is considered doing well for a man and doing well for a woman? Why do we not have the same expectations for success? As a little girl, my mother used to say to me, "Susan, you can do anything you want to do, as long as you are willing to work hard enough to achieve it." Unfortunately, that is not the way it works in the real world. We are indoctrinated over time via internal and external messages that impose limitations and diminish our expectations. Success and power begin with your own personal expectations of success.

Two Hundred Years and We Haven't Arrived

Did you know women have been an integral part of the workforce in the United States since colonial days? When our ancestors sailed across the sea to settle the New World, there was a severe labor shortage and every citizen was required to work. However, even though our young, embryonic country needed every able body to survive and prosper, women found themselves relegated to low-paying, undervalued jobs.

Women have made significant contributions in the labor market for hundreds of years. No one could deny the critical roles women played in keeping the economy intact during both major world wars. History tells us that women who entered the business world during these wartime periods enjoyed its challenges and were reluctant to leave. But, when the men returned home, society's message to women shifted. Instead of being encouraged to go to work, women were told to go home, take care of their husbands and children, and be happy. And for the most part, that is what we did.

In our society, men have always been considered to be superior to women in business. In the industrial age, when physical strength was important, men arguably had an advantage. As a general rule, men have greater physical strength than women do. But knowledge, intellect, creativity, and communications skills are the key components for success in the information age, and these skills are gender-neutral. Therefore, there should be no difference between men and women, but we all know it is not a level playing field.

In a desperate attempt to explain gender inequity, the crusty male-dominated status quo serves up heaping helpings of rhetoric about changing attitudes toward working women. Keep in mind that talk is cheap. Even today, the traditional roles of wife and mother are perceived to limit women in terms of their careers. A persistent and prevailing attitude exists that women will quit work in a heartbeat to get married and/or raise a family. However, there is no substantiated evidence that women, particularly executive women, leave the business world for those reasons. In fact, a 1995 Catalyst research survey found 83 percent of new mothers returned to the labor force within six months after childbirth, and only 17 percent quit the workforce altogether. As for senior female executives, 72 percent were married and 64 percent had children.[1] Forty percent of women in the workforce have children under the age of eighteen according to the Bureau of Labor Statistics.[2]

Unfortunately, here's where women begin to give away their power because we do very little to dispel the myths. For example, a November 1997 *Wall Street Journal* article indicated that when women resign from a company, they often conceal and distort their real reasons for leaving. If they are moving to a better opportunity, they play it down or do not mention it at all because they do not want to be disloyal. As a result, women leave the impression that they are quitting their careers entirely. The article also stated that research revealed many women actually inferred they were leaving the workforce to devote themselves full-time to their families when they were taking new jobs, oftentimes with a competitor. In other words, it is that inbred "good girl" behavior.

Moreover, the antiquated "women belong at home with their families" attitude further perpetuates the myth that women cannot accept job transfers or be relocated. An alarming number of male managers use this myth as an explanation for not offering career-enhancing opportunities to their female employees. Once at a dinner party, I found myself in the midst of a heated discussion with several men, all from the same company, who adamantly argued that women will not relocate and that is why their companies had so few women in high-level positions. Finally, I asked these men if they had actually ever offered a move to one of their female subordinates. With condescending smirks on their faces, they said no. When I inquired as to why, they explained that it would be a waste of time because they already knew the answer. I wanted to scream and throw a plate of food at them. However, because I did not want to embarrass our hostess, I bit my tongue and tactfully changed the subject. The moral of this story is that very few successful women say that combining family and career has ever prevented them from accepting a job change or even relocating, but we definitely have an image problem.

Corporate America is quick to point to the increased number of women in middle management positions as evidence that things are improving for women. To make the current state of affairs more palatable, an analogy is made to a pipeline that is supposedly filling up with capable and qualified women. Therefore, the story goes, it is only a matter of time before women reach equality in the boardrooms and executive suites. Yeah, right. Talk about propaganda. The pipeline is not filling up—it is already full. Women are squeezed in like a group of college students piling into a Volkswagen to break a world's record. For those of us who have been in the pipeline already, it is crowded, uncomfortable, and too often you get poked in the eye with an elbow.

Women have the credentials and experience necessary for holding top-level positions in their organizations. Today, women earn the majority of college and master's degrees. Professional schools comprise approximately 40 percent women, and that number is growing rapidly. Yet, women remain mired in low-level and middle management positions. To get ahead, women must not simply demonstrate that they are qualified; they must be better qualified and willing to work harder than men. It is much like being guilty until proven innocent. Men, on the other hand, are automatically assumed to be competent until proven otherwise—and sometimes not even then. More than two-thirds of successful women (77 percent) attribute their success to consistently exceeding expectations.[3] A survey of *Fortune Magazine* subscribers found that 77 percent of female respondents thought women need to have more experience or higher degrees than men when applying for the same job.[4] Amazingly, 43 percent of the men agreed. The survey also showed that 43 percent of men thought genders were judged equally when applying for a job, but only 20 percent of the women agreed. Sixty-one percent of men surveyed thought that women were satisfied with the overall status of women in the workplace, and only 44 percent of the women agreed.

Women are less satisfied in their careers than men realize. That is where your responsibility comes into play. Together, as women, we must do a better job of expressing our frustrations and conveying our disappointments. Fair and equal treatment needs to be more than rhetoric; it must be an expectation. If we do not do our part to help the process, then we cannot look forward to much improvement. Think about these statistics. The Feminist Majority Foundation's research notes that as long ago as 1968, 15 percent of all managers were women. Assuming that it takes fifteen to twenty-five years for a manager to become a senior executive, women today should comprise at least 15 percent of top-level positions. But research indicates that women make up only 3.1 percent of the senior executives at Fortune 500 companies. At this rate, it will take 475 years, or until the year 2476, before women reach equality in the workplace.[5]

Hopefully, this dismal prognosis from the Feminist Majority Foundation is inaccurate. However, women must collectively change the way they are doing things. If women persist in doing things the same way as they have done in the past, they are going to keep getting the same results—and that is not good enough. It is time for women to expect more, demand more, and be more proactive and aggressive in addressing workplace inequities. To truly enjoy success, women must leverage their power.

Same Job—Different Pay

Another serious issue for women in business is the wage gap. Throughout the history of women in the workforce, women's wages have been significantly lower than men's. Part of the reason is that women's jobs historically were mere extensions of their domestic duties such as childcare, nursing, sewing, and cooking. Undervalued at home, these skills are undervalued in the labor market as well, and as a result, women have been economic bystanders.

Discriminatory attitudes toward women in the workplace have been reflected in the strong opposition to equal pay for women over the years. The reason why this has occurred is hard to understand. As recently as 1923, the Supreme Court struck down the minimum wage law for women. It took forty more years before the Equal Pay Act was enacted in 1963. However, the driving force behind the legislation was not a desire to ensure that women's rights were protected; rather it was passed to protect men.

According to Claudia Wayne, an attorney and the past executive director of the National Committee for Pay Equity, "The Equal Pay Act really grew out of World War II when women went into the factories and took on traditional male jobs, and their pay was immediately lower than what men had been paid for the same jobs. A lot of places like GE and Westinghouse had written into their manuals that when you figure out the value of a job via job evaluation, if it was a woman taking the job, automatically knock a third off."

The concern, according to Wayne, was that if women were going to take traditional male jobs for less money, then when the men came back to these jobs after the war, they would be forced to settle for less money. Opponents of the Equal Pay Act opined that if you had to pay a woman the same as a man, no one would ever hire a woman and the result would be mass unemployment of women. That never happened; however, the legislation has not been successful in achieving pay equity either. "The problem is the majority of women and men don't work in exactly the same jobs, and that's why there is a need for pay equity based on skill, effort and responsibility. If it's comparable work then men and women should get paid the same," explained Wayne.

The Equal Employment Opportunity Commission and the National Committee on Pay Equity began looking at job evaluations that measured skill, effort, responsibility, and working conditions, and subsequently set wages for jobs based on the evaluations. "We found that even accounting for all sorts of differences like the fact that women might be out of the labor force longer than a man, there was still a wage gap," Wayne continued. "It was clear the gap was because of discrimination. However, opponents of pay equity said the gap was because of unidentifiable factors."

According to statistics, women make about seventy-four to seventy-six cents for every dollar earned by men. As you go up the corporate ladder, the disparity in pay widens. Executive women earn 68 percent of what their male counterparts earn.[6] Male executives have been candid in telling me that they have found women willingly to accept positions for less money. So it is a no-brainer for them when they are making hiring decisions with an eye on the bottom line. Why hire a mediocre guy when you can hire a bright, talented woman for less money?

Considering the current state of affairs, it is no surprise that many bright, talented women are fleeing corporate America to become entrepreneurs. According to a report issued by the Small Business Administration's Office of Advocacy, the number of women-owned businesses increased by 89 percent between 1987 and 1997, increased their revenues by 209 percent, and increased their number of employees by 262 percent. More than 50 percent of all new businesses being opened today are owned by women. Statistics from the National Foundation for Women Business Owners show that women now own an estimated 40 percent of all businesses in the United States. The nation's 9 million women-owned businesses employ nearly 25 million people and contribute more than $3.6 trillion to the U.S. economy.

"Many women business owners realized there was a limit to how high they could go in a traditional corporate organization. So they've said, I'm going to just go out and create my own organization," explained Sharon Hadary, executive director of the National Foundation for Women Business Owners (NFWBO). "For women, it's an issue of wanting to be in a position where they can influence the direction of the organization, strategically and culturally, and they didn't have that opportunity in an existing organization."

Once again, it boils down to expectations—expectations of

fair and equitable compensation. Leverage your personal power to get the results you desire because passive acceptance of the status quo diminishes your success as well as that of other people.

Reach for the Moon

"Reach for the moon. If you don't succeed, the worst that can happen is you'll wind up with a handful of stars." That is something else my mother used to say to me when I was growing up. Today, when I am faced with difficult challenges, I remember her words. To achieve breakthrough success in the business world, women must reach for the moon. We must expect more from ourselves, our government, and societal institutions. We must insist upon fair and equitable treatment and equal opportunities. We must take pride in our femininity while simultaneously learning to adjust to a male-dominated business world. We must challenge demeaning and patronizing attitudes and enthusiastically accept leadership roles. Most important, we must learn how to utilize not only our own power but the collective power of all working women.

Notes

1. J. Glass and L. Riles, National Science Foundation Study, 1995, www.catalystwomen.org/press/factsmothers.html, August 23, 1999.
2. Taken from a Catalyst fact sheet, "Happy Mother's Day from Catalyst," May 1998, catalystwomen.org.
3. Taken from a research report, "Women in Corporate Leadership: Progress and Prospects," www.catalystwomen.org/press/infocorpleadership.html, August 23, 1999.
4. Associated Press, "Women Not Happy at Work, Men Don't Realize," www.usatoday.com, April 21, 1998.
5. Taken from a research report, "Myths about Women in Business," The Feminist Majority Foundation and New Media Publishing, Inc., 1995.
6. Associated Press, "Pay Gap Endures at Highest Levels," www.womenconnect.com, November 10, 1998.

THE POWER OF A "GO FOR IT" ATTITUDE

"The truth about women and power is that people think we have it, but we don't—because we are not using it. Every woman must think this through for herself; everyone must embark on her own voyage of discovery. There are no guarantees that you'll be successful, or that you'll be loved, but if you have a vision and if you have the courage to pursue it, you can achieve a wonderful and meaningful life."

—Harriett Woods, former president of the National Women's Political Caucus

Don't Wait for Permission

In college, Ann Ross served on a fashion board for a large department store. As a result of that experience, she fell in love with retailing. "That's what I really wanted to do, but there weren't any women in good retailing jobs back then. So I became a teacher," Ann said.

While working toward her teaching degree in the 1960s, she held on to her dream of retailing. She applied to a business school, only to be rejected by the dean of admissions. "I took my transcript over to him and I said, 'I want to major in retailing, and I want to go to the business school.' He told me girls don't go to business school because girls can't take statistics and accounting," Ann recalled. "I was really upset. But I just accepted it."

Then, something happened to change Ann's perspective. She and some friends went to hear Gloria Steinem speak. "[Steinem] said there isn't any reason women can't do what they want to do. Her words resonated through me, and all of a sudden I realized I didn't have to get anyone's permission to do what I wanted to do. If I wanted to be in retailing, I could do it," explained Ann.

And Ann did do it. For more than twenty years, she owned and operated The Paper Warehouse, a group of wildly successful paper product stores. "I saw Gloria Steinem again after I had the stores up and running and I went up to her and thanked her for what she'd said. She said she didn't do anything, that I had done it. But I told her it was she who made me realize that I didn't have to have anyone's permission to do what I wanted to do. Gloria reminded me that the only permission I needed was my own and the belief that I could do it," Ann said.

Ironically, while she was at the pinnacle of her own business empire, Ann gifted a business software program to her alma mater's business school—the same business school that had rejected her so many years ago. A thank-you letter followed from the dean of the business school, who coincidentally was the same man who had turned down Ann's application to business school.

"He said in the letter that it was so nice to see women succeed in business. And I thought, 'You creep. You didn't think women could cut it in business school a number of years ago,'" Ann remembered. "I don't think he realized who I was because I had a different last name back then, but I never forgot him. You know, his words left an indelible impression on me."

To be a successful and powerful woman you must be prepared to chart your own course and not wait for someone's approval or permission. If you wait, you are a conformist, not a leader, and you will never be successful in achieving your goals.

Don't Wait for an Invitation

While vacationing in Cabo San Lucas, Mexico, a volleyball game broke out on the beach near where I was relaxing under a beach umbrella and reading a book. Both teams consisted of teenage boys. Shortly after the game started, two teenage girls approached and clearly wanted to join in. Shyly, they observed from the sidelines, waiting to be asked. The boys ignored them even though both teams needed additional players. I had to restrain myself from walking over and telling the girls to jump in if they wanted to play. They certainly did not need to wait for an invitation from the boys. After about fifteen minutes, the girls gave up and walked on down the beach. Just as they walked away, another boy approached, watched the game for a couple of minutes, and then took a position on one of the teams. He did not wait to be asked; he knew how to get into the game.

In today's competitive market, you are responsible for creating your own opportunities, regardless of your gender. You cannot wait like a good girl for an engraved invitation to arrive in the mail. More important, if you sense that you are not being invited because you are a woman, there is all the more reason to force the issue. Remember, you cannot win if you are not in the game.

Judy Zeilmann is a good example. Zeilmann learned early in her career how to get in the game. Today, Zeilmann is extremely successful. She is a partner with an international investment company. When you meet Zeilmann and talk with her, you get the impression that she has always been in control—one of those fortunate people who seems to know exactly what she wants and how to get it. However, upon graduating from college, Zeilmann accepted a position with a large banking institution. More than anything, she wanted to go through the company's management training program. But when she inquired about the program, she was told women need not apply. Zeilmann refused to take no for an answer. Her dogged persistence paid off, and eventually she was accepted into the program. Elated by the news, Zeilmann rushed home to tell her mother, but she was surprised by her mother's tepid response. "My mother said, 'Judy, why are you so excited? Shouldn't you have expected to be included?' I remembered her words throughout my career," Zeilmann said.

Zeilmann's mother stated the obvious. Women should expect to be included and given the same opportunities as men. When they are not, they should adamantly question the system.

For many women, overlooking discrimination in the workplace is a necessary survival strategy. We choose not to rock the boat because we do not want to be labeled a troublemaker. It is easier to go with the flow—to be a good girl—than it is to fight back. When we are passed over for a promotion or a big contract, we bury our resentment and suffer silently behind a smile. Inside, a time bomb ticks away, ready to explode. Not only are we doing ourselves a disservice, but we are cheating future generations who are counting on us to forge the way.

There is no one out there to fight your battles for you, and believe me, no one is going to hand you a great opportunity on a silver platter. You must be willing to ask for it. If you wait patiently on the sidelines observing the game, you will miss the boat. Seize the moment and make it happen, because power and success come from creating your own destiny.

Build a Supportive Team

You do not need people in your life telling you, "You can't do it." The most successful women that I have met have amazing support networks, beginning in their childhood years through to their professional lives. It is impossible to build a successful business or a successful career if you have surrounded yourself with naysayers. Rid yourself of the negative people in your life who are pulling you down and draining your emotional strength and self-esteem. You need a team of true believers.

A student in a women's entrepreneurial training class I taught is a perfect example of how devastating negative people can be. During a class workshop, she asked for ideas to help her get her business off the ground. Although she was a talented artist who painted home environments (things like ceramic tiles, murals, and furniture), she continued to struggle with her business even after ten years. The class offered numerous suggestions that were met with similar responses: "Oh, I can't do that." "That would never work." "I'm no good at that."

Frustrated, the class finally uncovered the real barrier to this woman's success. It had nothing to do with her ability or talent. The barrier was her husband, because he did not take her business seriously and constantly told her that she could not do this, that, or the other thing. Sadly, she bought into his propaganda and absorbed his negative feedback like a sponge.

Positive reinforcement is critical. Vicki Wicks is a successful investment representative in Lake Charles, Louisiana. She works in a world dominated by men. Industry wide, only about 8 percent of all brokers are women. And more specifically, you will not find many women brokers in Lake Charles. But, Wicks did not let that stop her. She knew she could successfully build a clientele.

"I never listened to the negative people. I've always surrounded myself with positive people. I also read a lot of self-help books. And my teachers and family always told me you can do anything you want to do," Wicks explained. "No one can put limits on you except yourself. Just stay committed and focused."

As CEO and founder of SBTV.com, Jane Applegate said that she has worked with some impossible people during her career and has learned how they can sap your energy and stand in the way of your success. "I just don't deal with them. I either give up projects or hand them off or refer them to other people or just say, 'You know what, this isn't working out,' and then move along. You've got to get rid of the toxic people in your life and make room for the good people who believe in you. I think if more people operated that way, we'd all be a lot happier," Applegate explained.

Find a Role Model

One of the reasons women fail to have higher expectations is that there are relatively few role models. When I joined the ranks of corporate America more than twenty years ago, there were many women in entry-level positions. But, if I looked up the corporate ladder, women were few and far between. It is difficult to visualize yourself in leadership roles when there is no one forging the way.

"My aunt was an institutional salesperson on Wall Street. When I knew I wanted to go into the brokerage business, I watched and observed how she managed her career, and I learned a lot. But, there aren't very many women in the financial industry, and it made a big difference for me to have a female role model," said Laurie Marchel, who helps develop and train investment representatives for a large investment brokerage company, and was formerly a Wall Street institutional broker.

Your role model does not have to work for the same company as you do, or even be in the same industry. If you are like Marchel and are fortunate to find a female role model in the same industry, that is great. But do not hesitate to look outside your industry or to choose a man.

Sarah Hudanich, a graduate of Cornell University with a degree in business, spent fourteen years with IBM Corporation and attributes much of her success at IBM to finding the right role model.

"I was lucky that my first manager at IBM was such a positive and powerful influence on my professional career," Hudanich said. "Not only did he teach me to become a better salesperson/businessperson, but also what a real leader should be. People work better for people they like, respect, and trust. You must have all three. He also took me under his wing, and as he moved along in the business, he made sure that there was always a spot on the new team for me. His philosophy was [to] always surround yourself with people that are better than you and you'll succeed. He helped me a tremendous amount in the early years."

Watch and Learn

Sometimes your role model may become your mentor, as in Hudanich's case. But, in reality, that is not always possible. For most of us, having a role model means paying careful attention to the admirable qualities in people we meet and incorporating those successful characteristics into our own success formula.

Catherine Garda Newton, CEO of Bearoness Creations, Inc. and former IBM executive, says that her father turned her on to the idea of watching and observing an array of people. "He said, 'Sit back and look at each manager. Then, write down what things that manager did very well and what things he or she could have done better.' From that list, I noted which things I was already doing, which things I wanted to do, and which ones I thought I should avoid. As a result, I had people I looked up to, both male and female, and I paid close attention to the different skill sets," she explained.

Barbara Wilkinson, vice president of external affairs at Southwestern Bell, agrees: "In any company or large organization, you need to look at the people in senior positions. So I approached it not so much as a male/female thing, but looked for people who were successful, who continued to be successful, and studied their business behavior, supervisory and leadership skills, knowledge, and areas of expertise. Even things like their decisions to relocate or move laterally for broader experience," she explained.

Women starting their careers today are more fortunate than women even only a decade ago, because there are many more women in leadership positions. Today, women lead two of the Fortune 500 companies. Oprah Winfrey's success landed her a top spot on the wealthiest Americans list. In Washington, D.C., women such as Madeline Albright, Aida Alverez, and Janet Reno hold cabinet-level positions. Two women now wear United States Supreme Court Justice robes, including a woman who could only get a job as a legal secretary after she graduated from law school. In 2000, for the first time, a woman, Elizabeth Dole, was a serious and credible candidate for president of the United States.

There are excellent female role models, but we need more. The question remains, however, whether the opportunities are there. According to Eric Segal, the chief operating officer of Kenzer Corp., the twelfth largest executive recruiting company in the United States: "My philosophy is that the road for more and more females occupying the number one spot in companies has already begun to be paved pretty darn well, and when they get the experience and reach the grade level, they're stepping up at a time when they will be better prepared, better educated and really have some role models to look at."

Look for Companies That "Get It"

There is no sense in beating your head up against a wall. You will never reach the top levels in an organization if it has a culture that does not embrace the talents of women. Therefore, the first step on your road to greater success is to make certain that you are working with an organization that "gets it." Look around. How many women and minorities are in leadership roles? Review company records on diversity, and make certain that you get the support you need to achieve your goals.

For example, a company once offered a senior-level position to me, reporting to its CEO. There were no other women in senior management, and while the management team insisted they really wanted a woman to fill this key position, my gut instinct told me that was not the case. One of the executives candidly admitted that one of his peers did not like working with women. But he assured me it was nothing to worry about. I could only think of the Shakespearean line, "The lady doth protest too much, methinks."

According to Eric Segal, "Smart companies finally started to recognize that if 90 percent of the buying public is composed of females, why the heck aren't they leading with a female mind. Avon is a prime example of that. Avon was a male-dominated company, and the saving grace was when they transferred Christina Gold from

Canada to the U.S. and basically led a turnaround. They recognized that female input was needed." In November 1999, Avon named Andrea Jung as its CEO. In response to Jung's appointment, Sheila Wellington, the president of Catalyst, said that it served as evidence that there are a few cracks in the glass ceiling.[1]

A few cracks, yes, but equal opportunity, no. However, enlightened companies are reaping the benefits. The Center for Creative Leadership in Greensboro, North Carolina, found that 77 percent of U.S. companies that had formal development programs, such as mentoring, found them to be an effective way to retain and improve employee performance.[2]

Smart companies demonstrate a strong commitment to the advancement of women when they create internal networking programs for women. For example, Southwestern Bell sponsors Professional Women of Southwestern Bell (PWSB). Founded in 1985, the program facilitates the exchange of ideas and information about the company and the telecommunications industry to enhance its members' effectiveness as professionals and their career growth opportunities. "The old boys network has been part of corporate culture no matter what company you are with. A group of us came together to identify what we as women could do to create opportunities for women to further develop professional skills and business contacts that would better prepare us for career advancement, including promotional opportunities within the company," explained Barbara Wilkinson. Today, the PWSB is a national organization with ten chapters and nearly fourteen hundred members.

Procter and Gamble used its marketing expertise to set market-share goals for women in management. At the time the program was implemented, no woman sat on the company's executive committee and there were very few female executives. Furthermore, women were leaving the company at an alarming rate. After five years, the program produced impressive and quantifiable results. Women at Procter and Gamble now account for nearly a third of the vice presidents and general managers in the company's advertising and brand management ranks, up from just 5 percent in 1992.[3] Also, female vice presidents and general managers run some of the company's most important businesses.

Dain Rauscher, a stockbrokerage company, sponsors an annual meeting of all 143 of its female brokers. The company pays all the expenses for this conference, known as the Association of Women Brokers. According to Patricia Ternes, who is in charge of the program, the women who attend the conference show a consistent increase in their production because they are shown how they can become a top producer, even in an industry steeped in male prejudices.[4]

At the St. Louis–based brokerage company Edward Jones, a similar program exists to help women brokers succeed. But the Edward Jones program focuses not only on enhancing the success rate of its existing female investment representatives but also on recruiting women investment representatives. Currently, about 13 percent of Edward Jones's investment representatives are women, which is nearly 50 percent higher than the industry standard. Yet, Edward Jones has aggressive targets to dramatically increase the number of women investment representatives within the next several years.

"This business is a natural for women because our philosophy is to build long-term relationships with our clients. Women are good at developing relationships. Additionally, there is no glass ceiling as an investment representative. If you perform, the sky is the limit. We really want to help women reach their full potential," explained Bobbe Suhocki, a partner in the company.

Establishing internal networking programs to enhance opportunities for women is not only the politically correct thing to do but a good business practice. Furthermore, companies that are forward thinking and insightful enough to create such innovative programs for women typically offer family-friendly benefits, such as flextime, telecommuting, onsite day care, staggered hours, and job sharing.

If your company does not have a networking forum to advance women, check out *Creating Women's Networks: A How-to-*

Guide for Women and Companies. This publication is a basic guide about how to start and sustain a women's network in the workplace. It includes practical examples and advice from companies that have successful women's networks.

Play to Your Audience

If you have not figured it out by now, let me tell you that men and women are different. Generally speaking, we have different decision-making styles, different communication styles, and different management styles. Slowly, business is beginning to recognize that these differences are not deficiencies. In fact, in the new economy a new business perspective, a more "female" perspective, has a demonstrably positive impact on any enterprise. However, although the tide is turning, the bottom line remains that a woman's success as a professional is still measured by the standard of the traditional white male model.

"Let's face it, that white male model has been successful and it has led to some economic and social success," stated Sharon Hadary, executive director of NFWBO. "So I don't think that we should reject it out of hand, but what's really important as an economy and a society is for us to recognize that there is more than one model. There are models that are not exactly the same, but they can be equally as successful. In fact, women and many people of different ethnicities have different styles of leadership, different styles of management and that, in fact, is good."

In many instances, women can use their natural leadership style effectively in business. However, employing one style exclusively is limiting and foolhardy. It is naive to pursue a "What you see is what you get" approach. To compete effectively, women must learn to adapt their style and play to their audience. We can build upon certain female characteristics that are considered strengths in the workplace, such as team building and consensus building, while incorporating, when appropriate, some of the traditional male methodologies. The end result is a much stronger and extremely competitive package.

According to Hadary, "If you are in a different kind of a culture you may choose to lead, manage, and behave in a way that's consistent with that culture. You'll get ahead in that culture because you know how to adapt. There are different styles for different situations and sometimes it's more effective to assimilate."

According to the Catalyst research organization, female executives and CEOs both agree that companies have a responsibility to change to help meet the needs of women, but it is up to the women themselves to change to fit into the corporate culture.[5] As noted in Chapter 1, one of the greatest obstacles for women in the business world is stereotyping by males based on inaccurate preconceptions. The only way to successfully destroy the barriers such attitudes create is to break with tradition, but that doesn't mean that you should start acting like a man. (Thankfully, the days when women had to act, talk, and look like a man to succeed in business are long gone.) However, you undermine your own success when you fail to adapt your personal style and play to your audience. The majority of the women who have succeeded in business attribute their success to developing a style with which male managers are comfortable.[6]

Use your common sense. Learn to read the audience and adjust accordingly for an award-winning performance. All it takes is fine-tuning your skills.

Notes

1. Dana Canedy, "At Avon, a Woman Is Appointed Chair," *New York Times*, November 5, 1999, pp. C1 and C18.
2. Susan Caminiti, "Straight Talk," www.workingwoman.com, September 18, 1999.
3. Tara Parker-Pope, "P&G Makes Pitch to Keep Women, and So Far the Strategy Is Working," *The Wall Street Journal*, interactive edition, February 1999.

4. Michael Hayes, "Distaff Dynamo: Dain Rauscher's Patricia Ternes Leads the Firm's Efforts to Empower Women," *Registered Representative,* August 1999, p. 56.
5. Taken from a research report, "Women in Corporate Leadership: Progress and Prospects," published by Catalyst, www.catalystwomen.org/press/infocorpleadership.html, 1996.
6. Ibid.

THE POWER OF 20/20 VISION

"The glass ceiling, where it exists, hinders not only individuals, but society as a whole. It effectively cuts our pool of potential corporate leaders by eliminating over one-half of our population. It deprives our economy of new leaders, new sources of creativity—the 'would be' pioneers of the business world. If our end game is to compete successfully in today's global market, then we have to unleash the full potential of the American work force. The time has come to tear down, to dismantle—the 'Glass Ceiling'."

—Lynn Martin, Secretary, U.S. Department of Labor

You Can't Fight It If You Don't See It

Nothing pushes my hot button more than hearing someone say that women no longer face discrimination in the workplace. The truth is that women will continue to face the same gender discrimination that they faced in the past, unless remedial measures are taken. In fact, I believe there is evidence that some of the progress women have made is silently and slowly slipping away. The June 26, 2000, issue of *Newsweek* magazine featured an article entitled, "Will a Woman Ever Become President?" The article profiled leading women politicians. However, in that same magazine, buried at the bottom of page fifteen was a quote from the Reverend Adrian Rogers explaining the Southern Baptist Convention's declaration that women should no longer be pastors. He said, "Southern Baptists, by practice as well as conviction, believe leadership is male." When statements like that continue to be made, what kind of message reverberates through our society? A damaging message that undermines women and prevents them from becoming equals.

Although many women recognize on an intellectual level that discrimination is pervasive, they may not see it or choose not to see it when it happens to them. This phenomenon is what I call the "gray-matter glass ceiling." It is a self-created, internal glass ceiling that you don't even know exists because it is part of who you are. Socialization, culture, demographics, religion, and gender stereotyping all contribute to your internal belief system and can result in your inability to see discrimination when it happens.

Gender bias is insidious. It transforms itself through varying disguises, taking on different shapes and sizes, and it affects every one of us at some point in our careers. Still think it hasn't happened to you? Stop for a minute and think about the number of times that you were in a meeting with a group of men and they expected you to keep the meeting notes. No one asked; it was just assumed. Or how often have you been mistaken for a secretary? You are not alone. Sixty-one percent of women executives say that they have been mistaken for a secretary at a business meeting.[1] Have you ever been expected to fetch the coffee? I certainly have.

As a second-year attorney, Bonnie Glatzer was brought into a major labor dispute by one of the senior partners at her law firm. He explained to Glatzer that he wanted her to handle this matter for the client because he was moving and could not do it. "When he told the client his plan, the client said that would work out very well because the union wouldn't think we were bringing in the heavy-duty lawyers. The union representatives would just think I was there to take notes. As it turns out, the client ended up staying with me for years. They always said, 'Bonnie was going to take notes, and she ended up taking over the negotiations.' But that was often people's first impression of me in my early years of practicing law. I wasn't perceived as a threat. No one assumed I was there to play a major role. I think much more often women are viewed that way so the woman has to prove her ability to lead," said Bonnie, who today is a partner with the law firm of Thelen, Reid, and Priest in San Francisco.

In 1999, when Carly Fiorina was named CEO of Hewlett Packard she said that she was amazed that her gender drew so much attention because she didn't believe that there was a glass ceiling in the competitive high-tech industries.[2] Her comment infuriated many women because only 7 percent of the executives in the largest high-tech companies are women, as compared with 11 percent in Fortune 500 companies generally.[3] Perhaps the glass ceiling did not impede Fiorina's success, but she is one of the fortunate few.

Blatant sexual discrimination where the boss chases his secretary around the desk is rare these days, although not completely nonexistent, thanks to federal and state legislation that outlaws such egregious and overt conduct. However, statutory language does not preclude the more subtle forms of discrimination. There are a myriad of clever ways to block women from the top without being obvious. For example, a company can give a woman the title of vice president, but limit the scope of her authority. Or a company might promote a woman, but then fail to give her the necessary resources or training she needs to succeed. Some companies elevate women to top-level positions, but not the type of position that will eventually lead them to the CEO's office. There are unwritten rules that all the men at the top seem to know and adhere to. Although these men know the politically correct things to say, with a wink and a nod they do something else.

In the federal government's glass-ceiling initiative report, several attitudinal and organizational barriers were identified that impact a woman's ability to climb the corporate ladder. These barriers included a recruitment system that relied on word of mouth and an employee referral network; a lack of development practices and

credential-building experiences, such as career-enhancing assignments; and a lack of holding senior-level executives and corporate
decision makers accountable for Equal Employment Opportunity
responsibilities. To put the report's results in nonbureaucratic language, it is the good ole boys' network at its best.

In terms of career-enhancing assignments, only 6 percent of
the Fortune 500's top corporate women have bottom-line responsibilities.[4] In corporate America, profit-and-loss (P&L) experience is
imperative for those working in top management positions. If a
woman is promoted into a job without P&L responsibilities, it is
likely that her career won't advance much higher.

Like many women, I was once in one of those "going
nowhere" jobs. However, at the time, I didn't have the skills to recognize it. When I was vice president/director of marketing for ITT
Commercial Finance, I learned that I needed to run a regional office
to reach the next level within the organization. The regional office
job was actually a lower level position than my current one, but I was
willing to relocate and take a demotion to acquire the necessary experience. The company paid for me to take the skills assessment and
psychological tests necessary to be evaluated and included in what
was referred to as the P&L pool. The pool consisted of a list of eligi-
ble candidates who were to be considered for placement when a regional office became available. Little did I know that, for me, it was
an exercise in futility. Even though I had one of the highest scores
ever recorded on the skills assessment test and had more education
than any of the other candidates, I was never seriously considered.
You guessed it—I was the token female. Even today, to the best of my
knowledge that company, which is now a division of Deutsche Banc,
doesn't have any women running regional offices.

No doubt about it, the glass ceiling is alive and well. Nearly
two thirds of the respondents in a *Los Angeles Times* poll of twelve
thousand women reported experiencing sexual discrimination.[5] Additionally, a survey released by the Society for Human Resource
Management indicated nearly nine out of ten human resource professionals believe women face barriers to career advancement.[6]

Women are not breaking through the barriers as fast as they should. The fact remains that more women continue to work as teachers, secretaries, and cashiers than in other lines of work.[7]

You Can't Escape It—Discrimination Is Everywhere

When we speak of sexual discrimination, we often think of mega-corporations with their bastions of male power mongers. However, corporate America is not the only place where you will find gender discrimination. At the Massachusetts Institute of Technology (MIT), members of the female faculty were systematically short-changed in areas ranging from promotions and salaries to office space and access to research money. Women professors at the school found that in addition to lower salaries and less office space, there were no female department heads. Furthermore, while the school granted raises to men who received job offers elsewhere, the school often let women leave. As a result of these findings, MIT raised women's salaries an average of 20 percent to equal the salaries of men as well as to increase the pension of a handful of retired women professors.[8]

A similar study at Washington University found that only 21 percent of the university's female faculty members had tenure or jobs that could lead to it.[9] Nationally, an average of only 26 percent of women fill the best faculty jobs at comparably large research universities.[10]

The president of the National Association of Women's Yellow Pages, Jan Scott, experienced the discrimination in academia firsthand. "I had been a flute professor at Southern Illinois University for sixteen years. I had a great office with a picture window and a grand piano. Then, they hired a male vocal instructor, and all of a sudden I was given my choice of closets in the basement to use as my studio. I couldn't believe it," she said.

The not-for-profit world has its share of gender discrimination, too. Well-known author and business guru, Peter Drucker claims that leaders of well-run nonprofit organizations are likely to have greater skills than those of the CEO of a for-profit business.[11] He bases his observation on the fact that the director of a nonprofit relies on volunteers who may or may not fulfill their commitments. Therefore, the director must be able to motivate and inspire—cajoling each volunteer to see the vision and goals of the organization. Arguably, most of the volunteer coordination originates at the local level of not-for-profit agencies. And who heads the local efforts? Women do. However, very few women rise to the top of national organizations.

Karen Harriman, a twenty-five-year veteran of the not-for-profit industry, believes most national nonprofit organizations are structured so that the national or home office executive staff is predominantly male, while the field or local division/chapter executive staff is predominantly female. "Many of the professionals in the nonprofit field have a theory that the reasoning behind this structure has to do with the belief that men are better at business and management, therefore they are more qualified to head and lead the organizations. While it is believed that women are better at nurturing and that is best for cultivating local relationships and building strong volunteer bases in the field," Harriman explained. "For those of us who have been in leadership positions in the industry for fifteen-plus years, this situation seems like discrimination and ignorance in its finest form."

According to Harriman, who today serves as vice president of marketing and development for a regional health care company when you look at some of the exceptions where a woman is a CEO of a national not-for-profit organization, a pattern develops. Most women come into the CEO position as the savior, after the organization has experienced the wrath of the public because of ethical or moral issues, such as spending public donations on extravagant CEO salaries and perks.

Gender bias may be more prevalent in certain geographic areas according to Kim Calero, past president of the National Association of Female Executives and currently president of Successful Business Strategies Group, LLC. "There are some geographical areas where acceptance is moving faster than others. When I speak at events, or meet with corporate managers, depending on the cities, the feedback and comments truly reflect the culture for the workplace. Some take our interest and concerns seriously, some don't," said Calero. "There is a male population out there thinking [that] current statistics and women-focused publications take information and twist it to [their] best interest versus being factual. We have come a long way, and the change in the marketplace is certainly moving forward, but we need to address the geographic differences to continue to move in a forward direction."

Even women entrepreneurs, many of whom left corporate America to escape the glass ceiling, can't entirely avoid the impact of gender bias. A University of Texas study showed that women entrepreneurs with equitable skills and experience gross less than men do, net less than men do, and still face discrimination.[12] Once again, the differences in men- and women-owned companies may stem from the good ole boys' network. Elizabeth Russell, CEO of Pine Valley Spring Water, says that men are more comfortable in dealing with another man in a business relationship than they are with a woman. "Deal-making is easier for a man than it is for a woman because of the traditional male relationships that are formed from boyhood. Women don't make deals the way men do. Once you put a woman into that golf game, it changes the dynamic. It's not the same golf game anymore,"[13] claimed Russell.

According to the NFWBO, being taken seriously is the number one challenge for women entrepreneurs, which negatively impacts a woman's ability to succeed. While performing consulting work for a financial company, I was asked to present a seminar on how to market to women business owners. Several of the men in attendance made it clear that they had no interest in reaching this market. Although I quoted impressive statistics about the market's size, they refused to listen. Finally, one man admitted to me that he didn't believe the numbers were correct because, in his opinion, women were only in business so that their husbands could get a tax write-off and give their wives something to do.

"There is an attitude that their businesses aren't 'real' businesses. That they are just a hobby or something. I know women who have $20 million companies who still struggle with that attitude," said Sharon Hadary, executive director of NFWBO.

Linda Alvarado is one of three general contractors who worked to build Denver's football stadium. Her contracting company is worth about $37 million, and she is also one of the owners of the Colorado Rockies baseball team.[14] When Linda started her company in this male-dominated industry, she wasn't taken seriously at first. In fact, she signed her first bid with initials to hide the fact that she was a woman. "What I wanted to do was negotiate a contract," remembered Alvarado. "In reality, they wanted to date me."[15]

The discrimination against women business owners is blatant when you look at government procurement contracts. Women entrepreneurs get less than 2 percent of the prime federal contracts, and less than 4 percent of the subcontracts. Measured by both the number and dollar value of federal contracts, women's participation in procurements comes up far short of their share of overall economic activity.[16]

"Is it reasonable to believe that women's businesses in this country can provide only between two and four percent of the goods or services needed by the government? I don't think so," claimed Sherrye Henry, assistant administrator for Women's Business Ownership, U.S. Small Business Administration (SBA). "But somehow, the federal procurement market seems to be a nearly impenetrable fortress for women."[17]

To address this problem with procurement, President Bill Clinton signed an executive order in May 2000 affirming the administration's commitment to seeing that women-owned businesses receive 5 percent of the federal contracts for goods and services. This order served as a direct message from the administration to the heads of government agencies that they must do all they can to meet the 5 percent goal. The 5 percent goal was actually established by Congress in 1994, but it didn't work. This new executive order, however, spells out the responsibilities of the agencies and departments and establishes the Office of Women's Procurement at the SBA to spearhead this governmentwide effort.

Women business owners also have less access to credit. According to a joint report from the Milken Institute and the National Women's Business Council, women receive only 12 percent of all credit provided to small businesses in the United States. Furthermore, women entrepreneurs find themselves locked out of the venture capital market. Women-owned businesses receive only about 1 percent of all venture capital funds.

Discrimination is everywhere. It happens to women entrepreneurs, professors, lawyers, doctors, artists, teachers, musicians, and journalists. No woman can escape it. You need the power of 20/20 vision so that you can see it when it is happening to you. Remember, if it looks like a duck, walks like a duck, and quacks like a duck—it's a duck.

Watch out for Men Who Still Don't "Get It"

You can conduct all the sensitivity workshops you want. You can illustrate appropriate and inappropriate behaviors in the workplace. You can issue strict sexual harassment guidelines. But no matter what measures you take, some men still don't get it. I have been called honey and sweetie by opposing counsel in the courtroom before a judge. A national account manager whom I outranked introduced me to a major customer by commenting, "We bring Susan along for decoration." And when I was twenty-five, a high-ranking married man who was more than fifty years old stopped me one evening as I was leaving work, backed me up against a wall, tried to kiss me, and told me he thought he loved me.

Maybe these guys all thought that they were irresistible or maybe they were on a power trip—who knows. The problem is they pop up everywhere, and as a result, very few women can say they've never been sexually harassed in their careers. Therefore, it is impossible to talk about gender discrimination without also addressing sexual harassment.

"Inequality is not always measured in dollars or promotions; often it means experiencing the humiliation, the fear or simply the nuisance of sexual harassment," said Sherrye Henry in her book, *The Deep Divide: Why American Women Resist Equality.*

Sexual harassment is far more prevalent in the business world than people realize. Studies show that nearly 90 percent of women in the U.S. workforce have been the victims of some form of sexual harassment on the job.[18] It can be subtle and seemingly innocuous, such as calling female coworkers honey or sweetie, or it can be threatening and intimidating. The concern is that if it is so prevalent, why don't we hear more about it? The answer is that women do not talk about it. It is a taboo subject because too often it is the accuser, not the harasser, who comes under attack.

Remember when Anita Hill stepped forward to testify in the Clarence Thomas hearings. She subjected herself to public ridicule because many people did not believe her, including the all-male Senate Judiciary Committee. She courageously placed her reputation and professional career on the line to do what she thought was right.

Personally, I empathize with and admire Anita Hill. For several years, I suffered at the hands of a sexual harasser who made my life a living hell. Yet, I chose not to file formal charges because I didn't want to subject myself to public humiliation and emotional trauma. I now regret my decision. That is why I am passionate about asking other women who are or have previously been harassed to talk about the experience and to support each other. We can't allow society to make the victim the villain in sexual harassment cases. However, unless we start talking, society will continue to close its eyes to sexual harassment.

Sexual harassment is much more than a legal issue. The pain it causes can traumatize a woman's life. More than 90 percent of sexually harassed women suffer from some debilitating stress reaction, including anxiety, depression, headaches, sleep disorders, weight loss or gain, nausea, lowered self-esteem, and sexual dysfunction.[19]

Additionally, the experience can impact a woman financially. A study of federal employees reported that sexually harassed women collectively lose $4.4 million in wages and 973,000 hours in unpaid leave each year.[20]

One of the reasons why sexual harassment claims are met with skepticism is that they are difficult to prove. Frequently, the harassment occurs between a supervisor and a subordinate and it boils down to a he said/she said scenario. Studies show that over half of all sexual harassers are the direct supervisors of their target, and that supervisors are more likely to engage in and get away with more severe forms of harassment.[21] They can get away with it because they have the power of the organization behind them, and as a result, the victim is unlikely to complain. A woman who is harassed fears retaliation or dismissal if she speaks up, so she silently endures the situation or quits and looks for work elsewhere. Either way, she is the one who looses.

Companies that ignore or condone sexual harassment often find themselves paying out large settlements. Large corporations lose about $6.7 million a year because of issues related to sexual harassment, such as low morale and absenteeism.[22] This figure does not include litigation costs where one case can cost millions. For example, the U.S. Equal Employment Opportunity Commission (EEOC) reached a settlement with Ford Motor Company for nearly $8 million in damages to be paid to female employees alleged to have been victimized by sexual harassment, racial harassment, harassment on the basis of sex, and retaliation for complaining to management about harassment.[23] In 1998, Mitsubishi made a record payment of $34 million to women on its assembly line in a sexual harassment case.[24]

Not only does sexual harassment have a bottom-line impact, but also companies that tolerate harassment, in essence, support the intimidation and demoralization of their women employees. Sexual harassment is nothing more than abuse. And abuse is abuse no matter where it occurs. That is why I refer to sexual harassment as the domestic violence of the business world. According to Claudia

Wayne, former head of the women's rights clinic at Antioch Law School and professor of family law, women's rights, and employment discrimination, "Violence, whether it's in the home, on the streets, or in the workplace is an issue of power. It is an issue of keeping women down. It is terrorizing."

A number of years ago, domestic violence victims found themselves isolated because of a psychological misconception that causes the victim to feel as though she deserves the abusive treatment. The feeling that it was their fault is the same feeling experienced by women who have been the victims of sexual harassment. Because these victims feel responsible, they would rather keep the secret than expose the perpetrator.

Fortunately, today there are agencies, educational programs, and support groups to aid and assist domestic violence victims. We need the same type of support for women who have been abused in the workplace. There should be public forums where women can freely discuss their experiences while raising public awareness. Women can learn from each other if they don't insist on handling the problem on their own. If we put up with, hide, and ignore abuse, then we are saying that it is okay—and there is nothing okay about it.

Empower Yourself—Know Your Rights

"There are some men who just don't get the message, and they take liberties. In their head they think you'd want to go to bed with them because they're gorgeous or powerful or whatever," explained Karen Harriman, who worked in the not-for-profit industry for many years. "I had one of our lead volunteers hit on me. But I drew the line right up front. I turned my back on him, and I said you really need to go away and find out who you really are because I don't' like the person I'm looking at right now."

First and foremost, to combat sexual harassment, you must make it perfectly clear to the harasser that the behavior is unwelcome. In doing so, you can sometimes stop a potential harasser in his tracks. "Once the line of expected appropriate behavior is drawn, I have found that men will respect that information or line," stated Harriman. "When I mentor younger women I stress the importance of directness and appropriate business behavior. If a woman doesn't make expected behavior clear from the very beginning of a relationship, she is asking for trouble."

Marsha Serlin, CEO of United Scrap Metal in Cicero, Illinois, knows exactly how to put a harasser in his place. She refused to allow a potential client to intimidate her, even though at the time, she was just getting started in business and needed to close the deal. "It was right after I was divorced," remembered Serlin. "I had a guy who said he wouldn't do business with me unless I went to dinner with him. I said, 'I forget it. I guess we can't do business.' But I did do business with him eventually, and I think it was just a way to see if he could get me. It's kind of a game for some men. You just have to make sure the lines are clearly drawn, and you can't freak out over worrying about not getting the business. Forget it."

Humor can sometimes work as a good deflector as long as your message comes through clearly. During a customer presentation for a group of high-level executives, Catherine Garda Newton, who at the time was an executive with IBM, was interrupted when a man poked his head in the room and said, "Catherine, I'll give you all the rum you can drink and $30,000 a year to come live with me."

Stunned, the first thought that flashed through her head was that $30,000 a year wouldn't be enough. But, her second thought was that she didn't like rum, so she retorted, "Sorry, I only drink bourbon." All the men in the room cracked up and applauded her creative put-down.

Know the Appropriate Steps

If you are unsuccessful at deterring your harasser, then you should know what alternative courses are available to you. Read your company's employee manual and understand what its sexual harassment policy is. If there is no written manual, talk to someone in the human resources department. Your organization should offer a formal process for filing a complaint.

"Most companies now, at least those of any size, have complaint procedures and somebody you can go and complain to," explained Bonnie Glatzer. "Don't hesitate to make the complaint. Make it in writing if that's what the procedure requires. I would certainly not advise anybody for the sake of their career to just endure it because that can have devastating psychological consequences."

Make your complaint in a timely fashion. If you wait, your motives may be questioned. Most companies will take the necessary steps to ensure that your situation is resolved in an appropriate fashion. If your employer refuses to help you, you can file a formal complaint with the EEOC or similar state agency. If after the EEOC investigates you still aren't satisfied, you can take your case to court.

"Large punitive damage awards have really heightened everybody's awareness," stated Glatzer. "But, not everybody has the emotional strength to pursue litigation. Lots of women just quit and go off into the sunset. You need to protect yourself first personally and then you try to make the right steps professionally."

Women fear they are going to be labeled as well as losing their jobs. Both are valid concerns. Therefore, make sure you are comfortable with your decision and that you have thought through the consequences.

Can an employer blackball or fire you for filing a sexual harassment complaint? Legally, the answer is no. If an employer takes negative employment actions against you as the result of a complaint, it is considered retaliation. The problem is that retaliation is a difficult claim to prove.

The reality is that as a practical matter retaliation may occur, and that's something you must consider. Ask yourself these questions. Do you want to get back at the company or the person who harassed you and prove your point through litigation? Is that worth whatever retaliation you might endure? If you ultimately decide to pursue litigation against your former employer, be honest with potential new employers. Today, companies recognize that mistakes can happen, and as long as you are forthcoming about the pending litigation they should understand.

Document Everything

The key to a successful resolution of a sexual harassment complaint is documentation. Sexual harassment claims are difficult to prove because there usually aren't any witnesses. Keep a journal in which you include notes of various encounters. Make certain that you include dates and times, which adds to your credibility. Memorialize your conversations with the harasser in writing when appropriate, and don't be afraid to tell your coworkers.

Consider slipping a voice-activated tape recorder into your blazer pocket when you are going to be with the harasser. While the recorded conversation may not be admissible in a court of law, it certainly helps when you lodge an internal complaint. So the bottom line is—document, document, and document.

Find the Men Who Are in Your Corner

Sometimes it's surprising to discover who your ally will be in a battle. In the war against sexual discrimination and sexual harassment, older men often are your strongest advocates. These men, many of whom were guilty of discriminatory actions in their younger days, now have daughters coming up through the ranks. They want their daughters to have opportunities and to be able to achieve their dreams. Because most of these men had wives who did not work outside the home, they didn't take women seriously in the workplace. But now it's a different story because we are talking about their "little girls."

"These older men have daughters they have financed through expensive colleges and graduate schools and even if they didn't take their wives seriously because their wives became homemakers, they have started thinking of their daughters as professionals," explained Bonnie Glatzer. "They become attuned to some of the issues impacting women. I've had clients and senior partners talk to me about career issues their daughters are facing, and they want my advice as to what to tell their daughters."

According to Carolyn Elman, executive director of the American Business Women's Association, "These older men sit around the Sunday dinner table and other family meals, and they hear their daughters talk about how awful it is. So they do have a better understanding. A more personal understanding of how it is out there."

Unfortunately, it appears that men in their thirties may be more prejudiced than men over forty-five. The younger generation of men seems to be clinging to many of the negative attitudes toward women that were prevalent in the past. Studies suggest that as women increase in number and get closer to the top, the resistance from men hardens, and discrimination becomes more blatant.[25]

Be Part of the Solution, Not the Problem

When it comes to issues surrounding the glass ceiling, such as sexual harassment and sexual discrimination, you can't ignore the problem and hope that it will eventually go away. Although most men do not perceive the glass ceiling as a real issue, 61 percent of women say they have little or no ability to advance.[26] Therefore, to break through the barrier, we must do everything in our power to encourage businesses to provide equal career advancement opportunities to women. We aren't asking for special treatment—we are demanding fair and equitable treatment.

Don't be guilty of burying your head in the sand. Keep your eyes open. Take a proactive approach and speak up when you see workplace inequities or evidence of sexual harassment. Secretary of

State Madeline Albright said that women cannot maintain a naive certainty that everything will turn out for the best. "And we [as women] are determined to see that every woman and girl has her chance, that abuse and exploitation are opposed, and that doors of opportunity are opened and ceilings that limit advancement are smashed."[27]

Acknowledging that gender bias has a direct impact on your personal success, that it is not simply a rhetorical discussion, is an important first step in your personal journey toward greater success and power. Once you break through the limiting clutches of denial, utilize power to collaborate with other women to fight for a performance-based business environment that fully and fairly values women as equal partners in American life.

Notes

1. *The Wall Street Journal*/Gallup poll, as cited in "The Glass Ceiling," www.feminist.org/research/ewb glass.html, August 3, 1999.
2. Tom Brokaw, "Breaking the Glass Ceiling," NBC News, www.msnbc.com/news/335580.asp, November 22, 1999.
3. Ibid.
4. Susan Bowles, "By the Numbers: A New Group of Chief Financial Officers Are Moving into the Top Ranks of American Corporations," comen CONNECT.com, July 28, 1999.
5. "Empowering Women in Business," www.feminist.org/research/ewb glass.html, August 3, 1999.
6. "SHRM: Majority of HR Professionals See a Glass Ceiling in the Workplace," DOWJONES.com archives, June 28, 1999.
7. "Facts on Working Women," U.S. Department of Labor Women's Bureau, April 1999.
8. Associated Press, "MIT's Female Faculty Were Shortchanged, Report Says," *St. Louis Post Dispatch*, March 24, 1999, p. A8.
9. Susan Thomson, "Survey at WU Says Women Are Underrepresented on the Faculty," *St. Louis Post Dispatch*, November 24, 1999, p. B1.
10. Ibid.
11. Sally Helgesen, *The Female Advantage: Women's Ways of Leadership*, (New York: Doubleday, 1995), p. 71.

12. "Women Business Owners Bump into the Gold Ceiling," www.advanc ingwomen.com/gold.html, March 2, 1999.

13. Lacey Burnette, "Breaking through the Glass Ceiling," *St. Louis Post Dispatch*, April 3, 2000, p. B13.

14. "Alvarado: Building Her Own Future," *NBC Nightly News*, August 16, 1999.

15. Ibid.

16. "Women in Business," SBA Office of Advocacy, October 1998.

17. Letter from Sherrye Henry of the SBA's Office of Women Business Ownership, May 1999.

18. "Sexual Harassment in the Workpalce," Equal Rights Organization, January 23, 2000.

19. Ibid.

20. Ibid.

21. Ibid.

22. Ibid.

23. "EEOC and Ford Sign Multi-million Dollar Settlement of Sexual Harassment Case," EEOC news release, September 7, 1999.

24. Gina Bellafonte, "Feminism. It's All about Me!" www.pathfinder.com/ time/magazine/198/dom/980629/cover2.html, June 29, 1998.

25. "Myths about Women in Business," The Feminist Majority Foundation and New Media Publishing, Inc., 1995.

26. "Working Women Count!" A Report to the Nation, Department of Labor Women's Bureau, 1994.

27. Secretary of State Madeleine Albright, speaking at the First Ladies' Salute to First Women's Gala Dinner, March 17, 1999.

THE POWER OF COMMUNICATING LIKE a PRO

It's Not about What You Say— It's How You Say It

The process of understanding the evolution of defined gender roles in our society and the concomitant prejudice is both enlightening and empowering. However, we must recognize that it is difficult to change these deeply ingrained attitudes. That is why it is equally important to examine what women do to undermine their own personal success. We have the power to take control of our own destiny and modify our behavior to enhance our ability to succeed.

Most women take pride in being good communicators. Ironically, communication is one of the areas where women frequently stumble in the business world. Men and women spend 85 to 90 percent of their time communicating with others. Your style of communication says a lot about who you are. It offers telltale signs of where you are from, your educational level, your interests, and your values.

Gender has a significant impact on the way you communicate. Starting at an early age, men and women learn different communication styles. Communicative behaviors that are considered acceptable for little boys are frequently frowned upon for little girls. Boys are taught to be goal-oriented and competitive. Girls learn to be open, to share their feelings, and to be accommodating. Many people believe that girls develop a style of communication that reflects their traditional role in society—that is, to be nurturing and deferential.

Whitney Johns Martin, the CEO of Capital Across America and a past president of the National Association of Women Business Owners (NAWBO), says she notices a difference when women contact her company to talk about borrowing money. "They discuss a lot of personal issues like a problem with their marriage or a problem with their children. But men are not as open about these kinds of issues. They don't bring the personal issues to the table. I can relate to what the women are saying, and I understand. To the men in my company though, that openness is an unusual style of communication."

Which style of communication is better—male or female? Neither. Both styles have distinct advantages and disadvantages, depending on the circumstances. The problem arises when men and women fail to understand and accommodate gender communication differences, and unfortunately, that is more often than not. Typically, men and women stubbornly cling to an exclusive style and never take time to understand the other gender.

You are probably familiar with the popular book *Men Are from Mars, Women Are from Venus* written by John Gray. Gray says the reason men and women have difficulty communicating with one another is that we originate from different planets—hence the title of the book. The idea that men and women literally come from different worlds makes great fodder for cocktail party chatter. But in business, it's no laughing matter.

Men and women may not come from separate plants, but we do come from different cultures, and we have different perspectives of the world. With that in mind, when you focus on gender communications you should depersonalize the situation. It requires an objective viewpoint and the realization that you are dealing with two individuals from separate cultures trying to communicate with one another. Communication specialists refer to it as intercultural communication. Intercultural communication is defined as "whenever a message producer is a member of one culture and a message receiver is a member of another."[1]

Linda Jacobsen, CEO of Global Vision Strategies, travels worldwide teaching business executives how to conduct inter cultural business affairs. She describes gender communications in the following way: "It's not enough to look at this as just a male/female issue. You need to begin to think culturally, and when you look at it from this broad perspective, you'll begin to see how the layers need to be very gently opened up. It's kind of like peeling the layers of an onion and trying not to cry. It can be a very delicate issue."

Therefore, to become a more effective communicator, you must begin by opening your mind and exploring the subtleties, nuances, and preferences of a foreign culture, the male culture, as if you were preparing to do business in a foreign country. Erase all the preconceived notions you have about how men communicate and avoid being judgmental. Pointing fingers and joking about how men just don't understand might get a good laugh when you're having lunch with the girls, but such behavior isn't productive. Male bashing is an emotional reaction that creates an us-against-them scenario. "I don't mind that once in a while. In fact, it can be a little humorous at times. But we can't wind up blaming men all the time. The traditional male style of communication offers a certain amount of stability. We as women need to be more well-rounded," said Barbara Dressel, CEO of Automark, an international machine-marking company.

Successful and powerful women are too sophisticated to play the us-against-them game. They recognize the need to mainstream and to adjust their communication style appropriately. I refer to it as the skill of accommodation, which is a critical business skill because it not only enhances gender communications but also facilitates all types of communications. Communication gaps occur as a result of a myriad of factors such as age, race, religion, and national origin. Learning to accommodate for communication differences gives you the upper hand.

Depersonalizing male/female communications is the first step. The second step involves examining your personal communication style to identify your weak areas. For the most part, women share some general communication patterns that impede their effectiveness in business communications. Identifying these areas and learning to adjust your personal style is an important element if you want to communicate like a true professional.

You are probably asking yourself why women are the ones who must bend and accommodate. Clearly, men should also recognize the need to be more flexible. The good news is an increasing number of men are interested in learning how to enhance their communications with women. That is encouraging news, but what incentive do men have to change since they are the ones in control? It now appears that their dominance is eroding. The percentage of white males in the workforce is decreasing, and soon, white males will be outnumbered by women and minorities. Nonetheless, for now, you have an opportunity to leverage your power and enhance your success by fine-tuning the way you communicate.

The skill of accommodation requires the ability to focus on the listener. Whatever you do, don't be guilty of gender generalizations. Keep in mind that not all women and men fit into stereotypical categories, so you should pay close attention and adjust accordingly.

"You have to switch the focus off yourself, and focus on the listener. You can tell by their body language and their eye contact and just everything, whether they're tuned in and they get it or whether you're turning them off or you're getting resistance. Play to the audience," says Iris Salsman, a principal in the public relations company of Salsman Lundgren.

Learning to be flexible and accommodating in your communications is one of those things that is much easier said than done. It takes lots of practice and a dedicated effort, but you will reap the rewards of mastering this skill.

Speak the Same Language

Have you ever had a conversation with someone where you really seemed to hit it off? You felt an immediate connection. One of the reasons you felt that way was because your communication styles were compatible and you were speaking the same language.

Perhaps you find it odd to talk about speaking the same language when the majority of people in this country speak English. But there are many words in the English language that mean the same or similar things. Additionally, we all have varied interests, and we reflect those interests in conversational content. So when you are communicating with someone and you want to connect with him or her, you must listen carefully so you can choose your words and structure content in a way that builds confidence and rapport.

For example, sometimes variances in language may depend on where you are from. What do you call a soft drink? A soda? A pop? Different industries utilize terms that basically mean the same thing. For example, a lawyer may be retained, while an artist is commissioned. As a sophisticated communicator, your task is to listen closely so that you can mirror the language. By doing so, you establish a bond with the other person and signal that you are familiar with the geographic area, industry, or business.

Additionally, conversation is peppered with content-laden messages that reflect personal interests. To connect with someone, pay attention to clues and use them to help facilitate your message. A classic example is sports. Men talk a lot about sports, and they use sports analogies and terminology to structure their messages. Therefore, to understand the conversational nuances if you are not a sports fan, you should familiarize yourself with sports terms so that you don't miss the meaning of messages such as:

"We're gearing up for a full-court press."
"I'm playing quarterback on this one."
"It looks like we're going to have to punt."

Personally, I don't like sports. I don't know a hockey puck from a baseball. Nonetheless, I have learned the lingo because that is the way a lot of men I work with communicate. I stay current on hot sports topics so that I can manage sports-related chitchat and sound as though I know what I'm talking about. It works. Speak the language and you will be seen as an insider—one of the guys—and your effort will be appreciated. Don't risk striking out.

The Saga of the Invisible Woman

Women are to be seen and not heard—soft-spoken, demure little creatures. Certainly, we have all encountered men in the business world who see women as little more than arm decorations, with nothing to add other than their beauty. For example, remember Senator Strom Thurmond's comment when Senator Mary Landrieu joined the Armed Forces committee: "We've got some pretty women on here this time."[2]

There is a media-driven obsession with the female sizzle but not the substance, as is evidenced by the superstar status of the Victoria's Secret models. Can you imagine becoming successful merely because you look good in your underwear? That is not the kind of success today's powerful women aspire to. Yet, the media plays the same old song over and over again—judge women by their looks and men by what they say. Do you remember how the press chronicled First Lady Hillary Clinton's hairstyles? There was no similar review of the hairstyle preferences of President Clinton, Newt Gingrich, or Ted Kennedy. The result of this excessive attention on women's physical appearance is that men are conditioned to focus on what women look like, rather than on what they have to say. They don't take women seriously, which creates a formidable obstacle for us.

Have you ever been in a meeting with a group of men and offered a suggestion that is completely ignored, only to watch it enthusiastically accepted when a man introduces the same idea a few minutes later? When I ask women in my seminars that question, there is an audible groan. Everyone has a story to tell.

As the first female named to a vice president's position with one of the country's largest advertising agencies, Beverly Berner found that her ideas often fell on deaf ears. "One of the men would take my idea and just shift it ever so slightly and all of a sudden it became a great idea, and I'd be sitting there thinking, 'Well where did you think that came from?' Sometimes, because of the nature of the creative process, I saw it happen to men, but not that often," she explained.

It is the saga of the invisible woman. Women are invisible because of personal bias—an attitude that women aren't serious players in the business world. Some Neanderthal men refuse to accept women as coworkers, bosses, or decision makers. Therefore, anything we have to say gets filtered through a screen of antiquated perceptions, and by the time it is actually received, it has little significance.

Donna Vandiver runs a multimillion-dollar public relations and strategic-planning company. By any standards, she is a successful business professional. As the only woman participating in a chamber-sponsored business group, Vandiver found she completely disappeared when the male chair began to solicit ideas during a brainstorming session.

"I couldn't believe it. He presented the problem and then started going around the table asking for input. It was an area where

I knew I had experience and some good ideas, but when it was my turn, he skipped me," Vandiver recalled. "My first thought was I'm not going to share my ideas with him. Finally, I decided to elbow my way in and make him listen to me. Before long he was writing down some of my recommendations. This guy is only forty-two years old, and it's hard for him to see women as anything but a secretary or someone to fetch coffee, and I just couldn't let him get away with it."

Women are out there, and like Vandiver, we can't let men get away with making us invisible. One way we can crack the invisible shield is to wield a more powerful presentation style. Earlier, I explained that women learn communication behaviors that reflect their role in society. They are taught to be soft-spoken and demure around the opposite sex. However, the business world is no place to be ladylike—whatever that means. The soft, breathy Marilyn Monroe voice might have its place, but not in the boardroom. It makes you appear timid, shy, and unsure of yourself, which impacts your credibility and professionalism.

Turn up the volume. Speak in a manner that commands attention. If your natural speaking voice is soft, there are exercises you can perform to strengthen it. Powerful voice control comes from your diaphragm, the muscle beneath your rib cage. Like any muscle, however, it needs exercise to enhance its strength. Have you ever noticed the thick waistlines on even the thinnest opera singers? That is because they have an extremely developed diaphragm muscle.

To strengthen your diaphragm, practice breathing deeply and pushing out your voice from your stomach area. You should actually be able to see your stomach expand and deflate. It may hurt a little at first, but as they say—no pain, no gain.

Voice tonality is another issue. Typically, women speak at a higher pitch than men do, making it more difficult for them to be heard. When you add a little nervousness and emotion to the situation, your vocal pitch can go even higher. A high-pitched, meek voice doesn't say, "I'm in control."

With some practice, you can learn to control the pitch of your voice. If you have access to a piano, find a lower note on the keyboard where you can speak comfortably without straining your vocal chords. Try talking while maintaining your voice at that level. Tape-record yourself and listen to how you sound. Do you grimace at the sound of your own voice? If you don't like what you hear, neither will your listeners.

Consider working with a vocal coach if you have difficulty with the at-home exercises. In addition to projection and tonality, a vocal coach can help you learn to enunciate better or rid yourself of an annoying regional accent. Local community colleges often have trainers in their communication departments who work with students interested in pursuing a career in electronic journalism.

Vocal inflections can impact the credibility of your message. An upward inflection at the end of your sentences sounds tentative. It appears that you are asking a question, rather than making an affirmative statement. Indirectly, it conveys a message to your listeners that you need affirmation. Confident, powerful women don't need affirmation. End your sentences on a lower pitch. You will sound in control and committed to your ideas, and people will sit up and take notice.

Avoid ending sentences with questions, such as "The company should have casual day every Friday, don't you think?" Why turn your statement into a question? If you think casual Fridays are a good idea, then say so. Women are consensus builders, and therefore, we have a propensity to solicit feedback and the group's support. However, there is a time and place for everything, and if you want to ensure your ideas are taken seriously, then you must be direct and straightforward.

Intimacy Doesn't Work in the Boardroom

Women like to talk about relationships and feelings. Our conversations are filled with personal details, descriptive adjectives, and superfluous words. For the most part, however, that type of intimacy is not appropriate in business communications.

This point became even clearer for me when I worked on a script for a corporate video program in which a high-ranking woman in the company was to be the host. Having never met this woman and not knowing her personality, I took a stab at drafting her remarks and e-mailed them to her. When she called me later to discuss what I had written, she said she was comfortable with the content, but she wanted to delete all the fluffy words. She and I went through the script and she deleted the superfluous language. After we finished, she explained to me that she attributed much of her success in her career to her ability to communicate in a direct, dynamic fashion.

Avoid using emotion-laden or "warm and fuzzy" words. Avoid such phrases as "I feel really good about that"; "I'm so excited"; "I'd love to help you"; "I think this is going to be really great." Focus on the real substance of your message. Structure your statements to emphasize the key issues in an affirmative way. Intimate language is fine when you're talking to your friends or your family, but in business, dynamic words demonstrate your expertise, project confidence, and demand respect.

Don't Dish the Dirt with the Guys

Knowing the personalities involved in a given situation often helps women to evaluate and make decisions. Conversely, men usually are not tuned in to personal details, so use caution. The behind-the-scenes gossip may seem irrelevant and irritating to a man, and he might consider you nothing more than a busybody. Don't risk tarnishing your professional image. Do your best to keep personalities out of the discussion, and stick to the facts.

Watch out about venting your problems, too. Deborah Tannen, author of *Talking from 9 to 5*, refers to venting as "troubles talk." Women like to talk through problems, and we want someone to simply listen. Inherently, men are problem solvers, so when women start droning on about an issue, instead of listening and empathizing, a man will try to solve the problem. So unless you are prepared to listen to his advice on how to fix your problem, don't bring it up. Call a friend, your mother, or a female coworker who will understand that her role is to listen—not solve the problem.

Personal chitchat should also be minimized when you are working with men. Most men are goal-oriented in their conversations, and they don't want to hear you discuss irrelevant matters. enjoy watching businesswomen engaged in a discussion because they comfortably transition between personal topics and business issues. Right in the middle of a meeting about the company's strategic plan, one woman might stop and comment on how much she likes the other woman's earrings. They'll spend a few minutes discussing jewelry, and then it will be right back to the nitty-gritty of the business issues without ever missing a beat. Women can do this because they easily shift between right-brain and left-brain activities. On the other hand, men are linear thinkers, and they aren't comfortable bouncing back and forth. Most men would find that type of conversation disruptive, and they would be frustrated by the lack of focus. Unless a man interjects personal chitchat, stick to the business issues at hand.

Watch out for the "But" Syndrome

This may sound like a crazy idea, but if you get rid of the "buts" in your conversation, you will be a more effective communicator.

Are you guilty of prefacing your ideas as I did in the previous sentence? If you do, you preface your statements with a disclaimer that says, "I don't have a clue what I'm talking about."

Society teaches women, as young girls, not to be bossy, too aggressive, or a "know-it-all." Did you ever have a bossy friend in your play group or in your class at school? She probably didn't have a lot of friends because no one liked the way she bossed everyone around. Girls are taught to share, take turns, and play nicely together.

In the business world, we try to preserve the inclusive, coop erative nature of our play groups. Because we don't want to be perceived as being too bossy, we phrase things in a less threatening, nondirect manner. Unfortunately, it is not only less threatening but demeaning and signals a lack of self-esteem.

"What we are really doing is putting ourselves down. It automatically diminishes the power of an idea. I used to do it all the time, and then once I realized how negative it was, I stopped," said Beverly Berner, a professional business coach.

Insecurity may cause some women to hedge their bets by using disclaimers. To avoid embarrassment, they begin by telling everyone up front they're no expert. Then, if someone laughs, it's no big deal.

"I have found that when I am feeling less confident than I normally do, that my communication style changes. Then I am not as assertive as I normally am. When my confidence level is up, I have no problem being assertive," explained Darla Hedrick, vice president of technology and product planning at SBC Operations.

To enhance your opportunities for greater success and to leverage your power, you must cure yourself of the "but" syndrome. Observe the men you work with. Notice how they say what is on their mind without using disclaimers. That type of communication style, regardless of which gender employs it, captivates the listener and lends credibility to the speaker. Don't give others the permission or power to discount your ideas. State your ideas with confidence.

Don't Wait for Your Turn—Interrupt

When Carol Daniels came to KMOX radio as a talk show host, she said she received phone calls from women who told her that she shouldn't interrupt the men on the program, and she was flabbergasted. Almost five years later, she says she still receives angry letters and phone calls from people who feel she is too outspoken. According to Daniels, she can't help but think that it is because she is an outspoken woman. She believes that her listeners may perceive that somehow there is something wrong with her—that she should take a back seat and let the man lead the conversation.[3]

Society teaches women that it is not polite to interrupt. Most of us were taught when we were growing up to patiently wait our turn. However, in business, if you wait for your turn, chances are you will end up losing your opportunity.

Research shows that during mixed conversations, men make 98 percent of all interruptions.[4] Most of the time interrupting us. I had never thought about this as a critical business issue until I heard Secretary of State Madeline Albright say that learning to interrupt is one of the most important skills young women can learn. Then, I thought about how many times I had missed opportunities because of my reluctance to jump in.

"If you're in a mixed group, everybody seems to pay attention when a man talks. I find women, even very successful women, often will be in a group and will let the man talk and defer to him even though the women's ideas are probably a heck of a lot better than the man's. It happens to us, maybe less than it used to, but it still happens," said Sharon Hadary, NFWBO's executive director.

As a successful entrepreneur, Marsha Serlin heads a $50 million scrap metal business. She recognized that she couldn't be shy and demure to compete in the male-dominated scrap metal industry. "I've been in this business for twenty-two years, and I'm probably too vocal. I don't hesitate. I interrupt. Probably because I'm very high energy and very impatient. But I notice most women aren't very vocal, and sometimes people take me the wrong way. Some male associates tell me I have a female body, but a male head. I take that as a compliment," Serlin explained.

According to the NFWBO, women aren't good interrupters because of their natural decision-making styles. Hadary says women prefer to listen and gather information before they speak. "This is often interpreted as she's unwilling to speak up, or that she's shy. Ideally, our society should understand these different styles so that we don't automatically interpret a failure to speak up in the first fifteen minutes of the meeting as being not involved. But women need to learn to adapt, and one of the things I've learned over the years is that I can speak up long before I'm really ready to. And that, in fact, if I want to have an impact I'd probably better do so," Hadary said.

Have confidence in your first reaction. It is unnecessary to wait until you have all the facts to respond. If you have done your homework and know your subject matter, your initial reactions are usually on target.

Keep in mind interrupting is part of a normal business debate. When watching *Meet the Press* or some other news program with multiple guests, notice the difference in the way men and women participate. Because men are more competitive, they don't hesitate to interrupt other guests. Conversely, most of the women are less aggressive, and if they do interrupt, they generally apologize as they break into the discussion. It is a rare occurrence to hear a man apologize for cutting someone off mid sentence.

Forget about the manners your mother taught you. You can do it! To ease the butterflies in your stomach, always make sure you are prepared. Ask for a meeting agenda in advance, as well as any background materials. Make notes, and if you don't understand something, ask someone to explain it to you. Consider doing additional research so that you will be armed with supplemental information. Most important, make a list of questions prior to the meeting. Rehearse your questions, and visualize yourself in the midst of a lively exchange. Role-playing is helpful if you can solicit someone to work with you. Good preparation means you will be confident and in control. And before you know it, you'll be interrupting right along with the best.

Drill Down to the Bottom Line

"When someone communicates with me, I want to know all the things you thought about. I want to know what your mother thought about it. I want to know what color you thought about making it. I want every detail. But, because I have to make a decision I do also want the facts, but I want a lot of extra information to help me make my decision," explained Vanessa Freytag, former director, women entrepreneur initiative, Bank One and currently president of W-Insight.

Like most women, Freytag loves detail, and detail absolutely drives men crazy. Remember Sergeant Joe Friday on the television program *Dragnet?* When he interrogated a witness, he would say, "Just the facts ma'am, just the facts." Men want to stick to the facts whereas women want to hear it all. We feel uncomfortable delivering the punch line without an adequate warm-up. But men don't want to hear the preamble; they want you to get to the point. If they need more information, they'll ask for it.

Men quickly tune you out if you belabor your message with unnecessary clutter. My husband starts looking at his watch impatiently when I get mired in detail—particularly if I tell an elaborate, long-winded joke. Keep reminding yourself that the key to effective communication is your ability to play to your audience—to deliver a message in the manner in which it will be best received.

Barbara Wilkinson joined the old Bell Telephone System prior to divestiture and at a time when there weren't many women in the management ranks. She began her career as an accounts payable supervisor and worked her way up through the ranks of the company. Today, she is area vice president of external affairs, and she says learning to drill down to the bottom line helped her to succeed.

"As you begin to work with managers at different levels, particularly when you're dealing at the senior manager level, nothing can serve you better than the ability to do the one-page executive summary. In bullet points, clearly state the issues, identify the two or three best actions or alternatives, make a recommendation and support why it was chosen. All of the background and details are sometimes too much. You don't want your audience to feel like they're drinking from a fire hose," Wilkinson explained.

Women who work in traditional male industries find that an

approach that quickly gets to the point is an invaluable skill. Mona Grelck spent a considerable amount of her career in the pesticide-related industry. She was one of only a handful of women. As the director of national accounts for Spectrum, a home and garden chemical company, she earned a comfortable six-figure income. Her business savvy helped grow the company from $25 million in sales to $300 million. She attributes her bottom-line communication style as an important ingredient in her success.

"When I went into that industry I realized that not only [were] the buyers all male, but all of the infrastructure was male," Grelck remembered. "Fortunately, I am very comfortable relating to men. I am more business, get to the point, give me the bottom line, let's figure out what the situation is, let's resolve the situation, let's come up with a plan and let's execute the plan. To me, these are compatible with male business strategies and thought processes."

A female mentor helped Heather Dorf to develop a no-nonsense style of communication. Dorf, who started with CNN as a college intern and today is responsible for field production at CNN/fn, learned how to strike a balance. "I am not exactly the same as she is, but I learned a lot from watching how she got to the bottom line and got it done. My mother is no-nonsense as well. She always makes her point and sticks to it. I learned a lot from watching her fight for my sister and me. I think I can go back and forth. If we had twenty-five minutes, I could take all that time to tell my story, or if we only had four minutes, I could nail my story down in four minutes," she said.

Focus on your audience, with the goal of making your listener comfortable. Give them what they want—no more, no less.

Why Don't You Say What You Really Mean?

Good question and one I've asked myself many times. Why don't women say what they really think or ask for what we really want? Instead of being direct, we beat around the bush. We phrase things in an indirect or suggestive manner so it doesn't sound like we are giving a direct command. This nonassertive communication style stems, in part, from our childhood when we are taught that good girls don't bark out orders. Compounding the problem is a double standard that views men who are direct and straightforward as tough businessmen but women as abrupt and abrasive.

From the standpoint of effective communications, the problem with an indirect style is that our real message is not clear, especially to men. Here are some examples:

Indirect Statement	Desired Response	Direct
It's hot in here.	Someone will offer to open a window or adjust a thermostat.	I'm hot. Would you please open a window?
There's my favorite pastry shop.	Someone will offer to stop so you can go inside.	That's my favorite pastry shop and I'd like to stop.
It would probably be a good idea to have extra copies of this report.	Someone will offer to go make the extra copies.	Make ten additional copies of this report for the meeting.

A mid size law firm asked me to present a seminar on effective gender communications at a partners' meeting. I was tentative about it because the audience was predominantly male. However, the presentation received rave reviews. A week after the program, one of the lawyers called to tell me about an incident that occurred with his wife. He said he and his wife were out one evening and decided to grab a bite to eat somewhere. As they drove by a Chinese restaurant his wife said, "Oh look, the Chinese restaurant isn't very crowed." Mindful of my presentation, he turned to her and said, "Now, that means you want to eat Chinese tonight, right?" He got a real kick out of understanding her message.

Most men don't take time to decode our messages—and examples of direct versus indirect messages could go on forever—but the area where women are most guilty of couching their true thoughts is when they have to criticize someone or something. Because most women do not want to be offensive or hurtful, they bundle the negative feedback in a package wrapped in complimentary remarks and tied with bows of encouragement. Then, they are frustrated when their message is misunderstood.

When delivering bad news, a direct, straightforward approach can reduce miscommunications. Mary Hwang, a student from one of my entrepreneurial training classes, makes terrific salad dressings and marinade products, which she hopes to manufacture and wholesale someday. Like many women entrepreneurs, she turned to the Internet for help, and she found SCORE's online business counseling. (The Service Corps of Retired Executives is a volunteer organization funded by the SBA. Its Web site is www.score.org, or you can find SCORE through the SBA's Web site: http://www.sba.gov.) The online counseling service matches prospective business owners with volunteer professionals who have expertise in a particular business or a related one.

"You can tell which counselors are male and which are female just by the way they respond to me," claimed Hwang. "I don't always like the answers I get from the male counselors. They are so direct. The women are much nicer. They are more encouraging, but the men just say what they think and that's that."

Hwang may have been displeased by the feedback she received from her male counselors, but I'm not confident she always heard the right message from the women. Because most of the feedback from the women included a lot of positives, there is a tendency to focus on the good and ignore the bad. If Hwang had flaws in her business concept, she needed to hear that in no uncertain terms before she wasted valuable time and money.

It is understandable not to want to hurt someone's feelings, but there is a difference between providing straightforward feedback or direction and intentionally hurting someone. In the long run, it is more considerate to be direct from the beginning.

"I find that people confuse directness with rudeness. Rudeness is a vehicle for hostility, which serves as a barrier for constructive dialogue, whereas, directness serves as a vehicle to initiate a dialogue," says Karen Harriman, vice president of marketing and development for a regional health care company.

When Harriman is faced with an uncomfortable work-related situation, there are a few rules she follows: (1) state the situation clearly—do not beat around the bush; (2) address the problem or issue in a professional manner; and (3) be honest, because honesty is the best policy. "These rules have become my signature approach to solving problems or issues so people who deal with me on a regular basis have come to appreciate and value my direct approach," Harriman explained.

Barbara Dressel runs an international machine-marking company and she says she doesn't sugarcoat anything. "Part of the problem is there's the time to be feminine and coy and there's the time when you just have to put that on the back burner. You can still be very feminine, but you can demand respect and interact without directly being hostile or unfriendly."

Break the Mold

Stereotypically, women are not expected to be assertive communicators. Thus, when a woman confidently asserts herself both men and women can be caught off guard. That can be good and bad.

Growing up as a tomboy meant playing team sports and competing with males, which was a great learning tool for Karen Harriman. She says because of her childhood experiences, she has always felt very comfortable communicating directly, one-on-one with men. "However, being a woman in business, my very matter-of-fact and direct style can make people uncomfortable and intimidated. I find that men and women equally have difficulty dealing in direct dialogue because they often are caught off-guard and unprepared for this type of interchange."

A male executive once counseled me to be less direct and assertive because he found that my style offended people. When I asked if he would make the comment to me if I were a man, he admitted that he would not. Therefore, I told him that I considered his comment a compliment.

Some women find assertiveness to be more of a problem with other women than with men. Jill Simons, a corporate investigator and bank officer at Firstar Bank, finds that her direct style often creates more difficulties when she is working with women. "I have found that being strong in my convictions, speaking directly and asking the tough questions, causes resentment among some women coworkers while at the same time creates confidence in me among men," Simons stated. "It depends, however, on the level of self-esteem of the women I am working with. There are those who, like me, are assertive, have attained a level of success in their careers that they are comfortable with, and they are comfortable with themselves. In those situations, we tend to develop mutual respect and work together because the other women are not threatened by me or resentful of me."

Never be afraid to break the mold. Regardless of the reaction you get, successful and powerful women know how to avoid being stereotyped. That is part of their success. The trick is to break the traditional female mold without being rude, boisterous, or aggressive. However, there is no doubt that the ability to say what you think without hedging your bets ensures that you will be more successful in reaching your professional goals.

Giggling Is for Little Girls

Women sometimes giggle, particularly when they're nervous. A little humor interjected in a conversation is good, but giggling is unprofessional and makes a woman look like a little girl—insecure and unsure of herself. Giggling also impedes your ability to be clearly understood.

Giggling is much like a nervous twitch, and the more anxious you get, the more you giggle. The laughter becomes a conversational filler when the person is at a loss as to what she should do or say. It also comes across as a weak plea for acceptance. If you want to be taken seriously and leverage your power, that is not the message you want to project.

If you are a giggler, it can be a difficult habit to break. Like any other nervous mannerism, however, you can learn to control it with a concentrated effort. I am a recovering giggler. Fortunately, when I was in my early twenties, a gentleman with whom I had interviewed for a job told me afterward that I had giggled throughout the interview and he found it distracting and inappropriate. Rather than being offended or hurt by his critique, I took it as constructive criticism and an opportunity to improve myself. Determined to stop giggling, I went to work. I solicited the assistance of my friends and family. I asked them to stop me whenever I started giggling. Soon, I began to notice it myself, and I learned to consciously stop myself.

If you are a giggler, you need to find a technique that works for you. Pinch yourself if you have to. When you try to stop, it will feel awkward at first, but soon it will become second nature, and you will appear more professional and confident.

Stop Saying That You're Sorry

How many times a day do you apologize for something? Pay attention to the number of times you say "I'm sorry," even when there is nothing for you to be sorry about. Women are constantly apologizing. They do it unconsciously. It is as automatic as saying hello and good-bye. Gender communication expert Deborah Tannen describes this phenomenon as a conversational ritual for women.

Ritual or not, when you say that you're sorry all the time, it becomes a form of self-deprecation. By accepting blame even when you are not at fault, you are giving away your power and jeopardizing your professional image. Men like to deflect blame whenever they can. So when you say that you are sorry, they are more than happy to oblige you and let you take the blame.

"For some reason, I've found that women in discussions or in group environments always apologize first. We say, 'I'm sorry, I might not have understood you.' Why do we say, I'm sorry? Why don't we just say what we really mean? When I hear myself doing that, I find myself thinking, 'Now why am I doing this?' That's something I think we all need to work on," said Sarah Hudanich, a former computer company executive.

Many women see apologizing as a way to settle a situation. They believe that if they give in, then the other side will too. But it doesn't always work that way. There are situations in which you should not be apologizing.

Professional coach Beverly Berner says that she tries not to throw it out there anymore. "Now I'm saying it only when I truly am sorry," she says.

Count the number of times that you apologize in a day. Pay attention to how casually you throw the phrase around. Once you are aware that you are doing it inappropriately, stop yourself before you say it. It is an admirable quality to be forthcoming and accept responsibility for something you've done wrong, but it is a character weakness to accept blame for things you didn't do.

Notes

1. Becky Michele Mulvaney, "Gender Differences in Communication: An Intercultural Experience," Department of Communication, Florida Atlantic University, 1994.
2. "Quotes of the Year: The Best and Worst of 1999," *Washington Post*, January 6, 1999. Taken from www.womenconnect.com/linkto/12231999_wcmm.htm, December 23, 1999.

3. Taken from a public debate between Patricia Ireland, president of the National Organization of Women, and Phyllis Schlafly, president of The Eagle Forum, November 10, 1999, McKendree College, Lebanon, Ill.
4. Pat Heim, Ph.D. with Susan K. Golant, *Hardball for Women: Winning at the Game of Business* (New York: Plume/Penguin Group, 1993), p. 139.

THE POWER OF PIZZAZZ: CREATING PERSONAL CHARISMA

What Is Charisma?

Some say that charisma is executive presence. Others refer to it as polish or finesse. *Webster's* dictionary defines it as a special magnetic charm or appeal.

Charisma is an intangible aura, and regardless of how difficult it is to define, one thing is certain—you know it when you see it. You can't miss it. It is spellbinding.

Charismatic people capture your attention the moment they

enter a room. Their persona is magnetic and captivating. Engage them in conversation and you will be charmed. Their masterful presentation skills can easily inspire and motivate you. No matter how stressful or intense the circumstances may be, charismatic people always appear confident and in control.

The power of charisma is so strong that women who possess it enjoy tremendous success—personally and professionally. They become political leaders, celebrities, journalists, and entrepreneurs. You enjoy being around charismatic individuals because they understand how to create strong human connections on an emotional and intellectual level. As a result, they are able to build loyal, supportive networks and their address files are filled with the names of people whom they can call anytime for anything. To find out whether or not you have charisma, answer the following questions:

- Do people notice you when you walk into a room?

- Are you comfortable maintaining eye contact when you talk to people?

- Do you keep your hands comfortably to your side when you are making a presentation or during a conversation?

- Do you like meeting and talking to new people?

- Do you make time to manage your physical appearance?

- Do you have good posture?

- Do you know how to graciously accept a compliment?

- Do you have a good sense of humor?

- Do you make others feel good about themselves?

If you answered yes to these questions, then you already may be one of the lucky few with a naturally charismatic personality. However, if you found yourself answering no to most of them, don't despair. There is no magic spell involved here. Charisma, like any other business skill, can be cultivated. Charisma is actually a combination of characteristics, but fundamentally it boils down to self-confidence and people skills. So here are a few success strategies to help you begin to create your own magic of charisma.

Create a Signature Look

The moment you walk into a room, people begin judging you. They watch how you walk, how you carry yourself, and they notice what you are wearing. These things may seem silly or trivial, but they aren't—particularly if you are a woman. Your overall presence speaks volumes before you ever say a word.

According to personal image experts, more than half of a first impression comes from your outward appearance. Your physical appearance is your product packaging, and product managers spend millions of dollars and thousands of hours researching the right packaging that will attract consumers to their product.

"Any marketing person will tell you, the first sale of a product is 85 percent appearance. The second sale of that same product is 85 percent quality and content. So, it's the packaging first and then what's inside second. So we're like cereal boxes on the shelf, and you have to ask yourself what's going to make someone pick you off the shelf instead of the other boxes next to you," explained Dr. Susan Scribner, founder of The Winning Way and fondly referred to as "The Etiquette Doc" for her seminars on business and dining etiquette.

Develop a style with which you are comfortable and that makes the appropriate statement about you and the image you want to project. Your personal style is as much about your business as your corporate identity.

"I was at an awards dinner for women entrepreneurs. The women receiving the awards were all very successful and owned big companies. But it struck me how poorly they were dressed. Some of them didn't have a clue. I couldn't believe that they could run a big company and not know how to dress appropriately. At least they could have hired a fashion consultant or someone to advise them," said Jane Applegate, CEO and founder of SBTV.com.

Defining your signature style may be a difficult exercise. Women who are like me and have been in the business world for some time can get a little confused today. Back when we started our careers in the 1970s and 1980s, the dress code for women was an austere business suit, starched oxford shirt, little ties at the neck, and closed-toe pumps. No one wore pantsuits or dresses. The goal was to dress like a man. If you wanted to succeed in business, you didn't dare venture from this formula.

Fortunately, women have more flexibility today. Now, it is acceptable to wear twin sets, animal print skirts, and sometimes even capri pants. You can actually dress trendy and like a woman. However, with so many acceptable choices, how do you determine the right style for you?

"I remember when things started loosening up in the early nineties," says Catherine Garda Newton, CEO of Bearoness Creations, Inc. "I told a dear friend of mine, I should write an article on how to become a transvestite because I had to learn how to dress like a woman again. I think now that women are allowed to be women it is important because it shows there is more of a recognition of the value of being female in business than there had been."

The key to the "right" look is to decide what statement you want your clothing to make about you and your business. Do you want to project an air of sophistication? Do you want to be a trendsetter? Is your goal to be serious businesswoman? Women's wardrobe selections are never neutral. Accordingly, women must choose carefully and wisely.

"When you develop your own style, everyone sees you that way and it becomes your look, your logo. I think it's important for any woman executive to create this distinctive presence because women no longer need to be neutral and 'blend in.' Of course, your look should be something that you wear easily and comfortably and feels right for you and the work you do. You often have to experiment, modify, and change before you get there. I know I did, but it's worth it," explained Flori Roberts, founder of Flori Roberts Cosmetics.

Casual business attire is becoming more popular, and like anything, there is a time and a place for it. However, you should never confuse casual for sloppy. An unkept, disheveled look is never appropriate.

"I certainly know the difference between when I work at home in a pair of shorts and a golf shirt versus putting on a suit. Your whole demeanor changes, and it's nice to have casual day, but often your attitude becomes casual as well. In a business atmosphere, you need to dress in a way that's going to instill such behavior. Also keep in mind that if you want somebody to do business with you, and be taken seriously, your apparel has to represent that," explained Kim Calero, president of Successful Business Strategies Group, LLC.

Finally, if you want to create a signature look that will cause people to take notice while at the same time take you seriously, avoid risky clothing choices. Younger women particularly have become a little daring with their business attire. Almost anything goes from cropped tops and tight knitted sweaters to short skirts with bare legs and sandals. Popular television lawyer Ally McBeal regularly shows up in court with painfully short skirts. On one episode, the diminutive legal ace was thrown in a jail cell for contempt because she refused to wear a longer skirt. It is difficult for someone to take you seriously if you are baring it all. You don't have to be frumpy and old-fashioned, but tasteful is always a smart choice.

Be the Boss of Your Body

Creating a signature look is only one step toward developing a charismatic persona. You must also be acutely aware of the message you are communicating with your body language. If your body language projects a lack of self-confidence, your credibility and professionalism will be questioned.

"There are patterns of nonverbal behavior that communicate

a given message. If in a given interaction there is a consistent pattern of positive nonverbal signals, it definitely is going to communicate a positive attitude," explained Dr. Marsha Firestone, a specialist in interpersonal communications and president of the Women Presidents' Organization headquartered in New York.

Your nonverbal cues can sabotage your success within a few seconds. For example, nervous fidgeting seems to be a common problem for women. Statistics show that women make twice as many nervous gestures as men when they enter a room. The result is that women look less confident, which is a difficult image to overcome.

Stand up Straight and Stop Fidgeting

For those of you who are fans of the modern-day Cinderella movie *Pretty Woman*, there is a scene where Richard Gere is whisking Julia Roberts away for a romantic night at the opera in San Francisco. As they are leaving the hotel, he tells her that when she stands up straight and doesn't fidget she's beautiful. Posture is so critically important. If you are slumped over with your shoulders rounded, you can't create the dynamic, charismatic image you desire.

When you enter a room, walk in like you own the joint. Even if your knees are shaking and your palms are sweating, hold your head up high and keep your back straight with your hands to your sides. Make eye contact with others along the way. Send a message that you can handle anything.

"When you walk into a room with an attitude that you're going to take charge and you feel comfortable with how you present yourself, the fidgeting almost stops," explained Kim Calero. "In the back of my mind, when I'm walking into that kind of a meeting, as soon as I walk in the door my mind is saying, 'Okay boys, it's show time. Let's play ball.'"

The same take-charge principles apply whether you are sitting in a meeting or standing while engaged in a conversation. If you are standing, keep your weight balanced on both feet and lean slightly forward because you will look interested and involved. Don't sway back and forth or fidget with your hair and jewelry. Keep your hands to your side, using them only for comfortable, appropriate gestures. When you are seated, sit up straight, lean forward ever so slightly, and keep your hands gently resting at your sides.

"The research shows that people who are fidgeting with their hands and their feet often want to escape from the interaction. It is a sign that there is some sort of intimidation or discomfort or fear. Freud says that even if your lips are silent, your feelings ooze out of you, especially through your fingertips," said Dr. Firestone.

Former IBM executive Catherine Garda Newton said that during her tenure at IBM the company provided a consultant to demonstrate the different ways women and men handle themselves. "For example, when a woman walks to the front of a room to do a presentation, she typically looks at the floor. When a man walks forward, he stands up straight, looks at the audience as he's walking as if he's saying 'Hi' and 'Here we go.' He establishes a confidence level with the audience. So I really, really try to watch my posture, and the image I'm presenting. It sounds kind of basic, but it comes back to modeling yourself after successful people, and I try to do that."

Flori Roberts explained, "You notice whether people have little nervous mannerisms or whether they seem contained and in control. That's very important. Overall you want to do business with someone who projects a together appearance and personality."

It is not easy to always be in control of your body language. However, perception is reality, and if others perceive you to be nervous and uncomfortable, then that is the image they will remember. The following tips can help you to present a confident appearance.

Stop Nodding Your Head

"Women have to stop nodding their head all the time. It's a matter of being secure and confident," stated Kim Calero.

When women bob their heads up and down, it reminds me of

one of those dogs you see in the back window of cars. Let's face it, who wants to look like a dog? Women nod their heads as a sign of encouragement, and as an indication that they are listening. However, when you nod your head, it gives the impression you are agreeing with everything the speaker is saying. In reality, you might not agree with anything, you're just being polite. Unfortunately, bobbing your head up and down is deferential, and it gives away your power.

Start thinking about the head nod the next time you're in a conversation and try to stop yourself from doing it. It can be difficult to do. You really need to think about it, and it feels unnatural when you resist the urge. But watch men in conversation, and I guarantee you won't see their heads bobbing up and down.

End the Head Tilt

In addition to the head nod, there is the power-depleting head tilt. Women tilt their heads slightly to the side when they are listening, but it is an indicator of submission.

"Jane Goodall, who studied the behavior of chimpanzees, identified certain rituals where the more submissive chimpanzees communicated their lower relational status through a specific series of behaviors expressed in the presence of dominant chimps. We also see that frequently in women. One of those behaviors is tilting the head. It is a sign of a status differential between the person they are interacting with and themselves," explained Dr. Firestone.

Resist the tendency to nod and tilt your head. Don't needlessly give away your power.

Create a Special Connection

Eye contact is probably the most important ingredient in creating a special connection with people. Charismatic people know how to hold your gaze in a way that makes you feel as though you are the most important person in the world. You can be in the midst of a crowd of thousands, but when they talk to you, you get the sense there is no one in the room but you. Politicians are usually skilled at this, and I've been told former President Clinton is one of the best.

Nothing is more insulting than to talk to someone who refuses to look you in the eye. Stay focused on the person with whom you are speaking to show respect and interest. Avoid the temptation to look at the floor or ceiling. By all means, never let your eyes scan the room looking for someone more important to talk to.

Eye contact projects self-confidence, and people like confident people. It is also evidence of integrity and honesty. "I watch the eyes a lot. The shifting of the eyes, what corners they go up to, things like that. A lot of people laugh, but there are programs that demonstrate that when people tell lies, you can see it in their eyes," said Linda Jacobsen, president of Global Vision Strategies.

Kim Calero agreed: "I find it very rewarding when somebody will look you in the eye. It's an honesty issue and/or a self-confidence issue. If I am considering doing business with someone that can't look me in the eye, I think twice, because something's just not right."

Someone once said your eyes are the windows to your soul. Eye contact allows you to connect with others. Master this skill and you will begin to enjoy the magic of charisma.

Put on a Happy Face

It's hard to stay in a bad mood when you put a smile on your face, and it's hard not to smile back at someone who is smiling at you. A smile makes people feel welcome and comfortable. But a smile should be appropriate to the context, otherwise it can backfire on you. There are times when smiling can make you look nervous and needy—particularly if it is overdone.

Studies show that women smile more than men. Why? Because we want people to like us, but a constant smile in business can make you look like a pushover.

"When I see women smiling constantly in a business meeting, I think they are either trying too hard to be liked or they aren't real comfortable with the situation. They don't look real serious about the business," said Bruce Baker, vice president of national accounts at Deutsche Financial Services.

Ironically, even though women have a tendency to smile a lot, they fall short in the area of humor. Research statistics reported in *Fortune Magazine* indicate women are being held back because they aren't very funny. Of the managers polled, male and female supervisors who used humor received a far higher overall effectiveness rating than those who did not. But according to the research, far fewer women bosses ranked high on using humor around the office.[1] Wayne Decker, a Perdue School of Business management professor who conducted the poll, said, "Many women may feel that using humor isn't appropriate for them, so they stifle their sense of humor in the business world. Humor can be useful in expressing ideas, making light of a situation, assigning tasks, easing tensions, or even communicating work-related information."[2]

A little humor works wonders, so lighten up a little. "Humor is universal medicine for problems," claimed Iris Salsman, who owns Salsman Lundgren Public Relations. "And that's true in business, too, because it forces you to take a step back, take a deep breath and see how absurd the whole thing is. If there's a business situation that is getting really tense or isn't going well or it's not going the way you want it to, you have to be quick-witted. Come out with the punch line. You just throw in something informal or off the wall to diffuse the situation. You just can't take yourself too seriously."

Flori Roberts, who founded Flori Roberts cosmetics in 1963, the first cosmetics line for African-American women, says she doesn't think she could have made it in business without a sense of humor. She believes you can see humor in just about any situation and finds it to be a great ally in dealing with people. "You particularly need a sense of humor as an entrepreneur because if you take certain things too seriously, and personally, you'll end up banging your head against the wall," Roberts stated. "Every day in business brings problems, and a healthy sense of humor does help you and your employees put it in perspective and move on."

Humor has opened more doors for Barb Gilman than any other trait or characteristic she has. "When I first started in the investment business with Edward Jones, I'd go out and knock on doors to meet people. It was about 112 degrees and when someone would answer the door, I'd say, 'I bet you wonder what a middle-aged woman is doing sweating all over your doorstep.' They'd laugh, and it broke the ice."

Don't use humor if you are concerned it might offend someone. Ethnic, racial, religious, or sexual jokes are never appropriate. And don't make yourself the brunt of the joke. That is a form of self-deprecation. Self-deprecating humor might get you a good laugh, but you are not in business to be the court jester. Always maintain your professionalism and self-respect.

Don't Put Yourself Down

"Men are taught to apologize for their weaknesses, women for their strengths."

—Lois Wyse, American advertising executive

Good girls don't brag or make themselves the center of attention. As a result, women have a propensity to downplay their accomplishments. And unfortunately, many women have been doing it for so long they don't even realize they are doing it. Even worse, women often emphasize the negatives. They put themselves down.

Being humble is one thing, but being stupid is another. There is a difference between being pompous and grandiose, and being positive about yourself. When you make a self-deprecating comment, it drains your power. Your listeners focus on the negatives and forget the rest.

"It's unfortunate because I'm afraid women really get hurt by that," said attorney Bonnie Glatzer. "For example, if you see a man in a hallway returning from court after arguing a motion, and you ask him how it went, he will inevitably tell you what a great job he did. It doesn't matter whether or not he won the motion; he focuses on the points he scored. If he happened to lose the argument, well then the judge wasn't very bright. It had nothing to do with his performance. You're supposed to walk away thinking he was terrific. A woman under the same circumstances will start by telling you about the one response she wished she had phrased differently. So even if she won, you walk away thinking she did a bad job."

There is nothing cute or charming about self-deprecation. You shouldn't forecast your weaknesses and mistakes or downplay your successes. We all have weaknesses, and we all make mistakes, but that is life. Successful and powerful women focus on their strengths and are quick to highlight their accomplishments.

Learn to Take Compliments Graciously

The inability to accept a compliment graciously is annoying, disrespectful, and a form of self-deprecation. When someone compliments you and you deflect it, you are undermining yourself and telling the other person they don't know what they are talking about. Does the following example sound familiar to you?

"What a lovely suit you have on this evening," a friend says.
"This old thing—I've had it for years," you reply.
"Well, that may be, but it looks great on you," your friend continues.
"Oh, I think it makes my hips look big," you say.

By now you are probably laughing because you know you are guilty as charged. Why can't we just say thank you? What difference does it make if the suit is old, or if you think it makes your hips look big? By deflecting the compliment in such a way, you have caused the other person to focus on the age of the suit and the size of your hips.

"As women we really need to learn to take a compliment

When someone says something say thank you. I think it's important that we, in our own hearts, accept and internalize that compliment," stated Sharon Hadary, executive director of NFWBO.

"It took me ten years to learn to accept a compliment," added Vanessa Freytag, president of W-Insight, Inc.

Don't wait ten years. Compliments make us feel good, and we all need to feel that way now and then. So, when someone offers you a compliment, smile and graciously say thank you; don't deflect it. Enjoy the gift.

If You Can't Say Something Nice, Don't Say Anything at All

"There is so much that is bad in the best of us,
And so much that is good in the worst of us,
That it doesn't behoove any of us,
To talk about the rest of us."

—Source Unknown

Trying to make yourself look good by saying negative things about someone else is the most self-destructive thing you can do. So many people, men and women, think that to make themselves look better, they need to make someone else look bad. Charismatic people refuse to lower themselves to that level. This is one scenario where being a good girl pays off. If you can't say anything nice, then you shouldn't say anything at all.

My father built a successful business because of his ability to be a friend to everyone. I don't believe I ever heard him say a bad word about anyone—even his enemies. As a result, he is admired and respected, a recognized leader in his community. From him I learned that if someone is unethical, unprofessional, or unqualified, you don't have to say anything, in time others will see that for themselves. Take the high road, and let nature take its course.

There is something good about everyone you know. Focus on

the good qualities, and if you absolutely can't come up with something, keep your mouth shut. When you make denigrating comments about another individual, you are the one who winds up looking small and petty.

Mind Your Ps & Qs

"Good manners are made up of small sacrifices."

—Ralph Waldo Emerson

Go to the library and take out a copy of *Emily Post's Etiquette*. Blow the dust off its cover, and acquaint yourself with its contents. Etiquette is not just about good manners, it is about good business. Polished social skills help you to create a positive, confident, and sophisticated image.

"We're in a new age socially. We went through a period known as the 'Me Generation.' People were very self-centered. Now we're moving away from that and people are beginning to have more of a sense of respect for others and more of a sense of pride for themselves. And that's what good etiquette shows. It says, 'I respect you and I respect myself,'" explained Dr. Susan Scribner, the Etiquette Doc.

Believe it or not, people do notice things such as your ability to properly handle introductions, appropriately shake hands, and yes . . . even your table manners. Some companies invite potential job candidates to lunch to see how they handle themselves. Do you know that your napkin goes on your lap immediately upon being seated?

"You're never going to go wrong by doing something the right way. If you call attention to yourself, be sure it's the attention you want. It certainly is embarrassing to choose the wrong bread plate and create a dilemma for the other dinner guests. That's not the kind of attention you want," Dr. Scribner added.

Etiquette is about being comfortable with yourself and making others feel comfortable, too. According to Dr. Scribner, knowledge builds confidence and confidence builds success. If your manners need a little brushing up, consider hiring an etiquette coach; attending a seminar on etiquette; or consider getting a copy of a business etiquette book like *Power Etiquette* by Dana May Casperson (AMACOM). It is worth your time, money, and effort to obtain that social ease.

Never "Wing It"

Charismatic people always seem to know the right things to say and when to say them. They don't pepper their sentences with "uhs" or desperately search for words. They are polished and articulate, which creates a commanding and powerful presence. But this enviable performance is not by chance, it is the result of careful preparation.

Rehearsing is the key to presenting a professional and confident image. Whether you are attending an important meeting, making a formal presentation, or networking at a business event, you should spend time thinking about what you are going to say. Do your homework. Know who will be in attendance and what will be covered. Make notes in preparation, and practice the points you want to make. Anticipate comments and questions from others, and be ready with a response. Create talking points for yourself so your thoughts will be well organized. If you spend enough time rehearsing and preparing, the words will roll off your tongue and you won't find yourself rambling on and on. Your conversation won't be cluttered with "hums" and "ahs," and your message will have impact and be credible.

In addition to rehearsing, you should shut your eyes and visualize yourself in the actual situation. Mentally picture yourself walking into the room. Think about how you will manage accessories such as your briefcase, purse, and coat. Imagine where you will sit or stand.

By taking time to properly prepare, you can ease your nerves and reduce the intimidation of most situations. Your confidence level will be high and you will be poised and in control.

Notes

1. Anne Fisher, "The Ha-Ha Factor," *Fortune Magazine*, December 9, 1996, vol. 134, no. 11, p. 220.
2. Ibid.

THE POWER OF A BLENDED LEADERSHIP STYLE

"A leader has the vision and conviction that a dream can be achieved. He inspires the power and energy to get it done."

—Ralph Lauren, fashion designer

A New Economy—New Opportunities

For decades, successful women who battled their way to the top were assumed to have slept their way there or they had to forgo their femininity and hide behind a cloak of masculinity. As I have heard many women retort, "I couldn't have slept my way to the middle," but nonetheless, that was the perception.

Today, fewer women are subjected to the "slept her way to the top" criticism, and more and more have found the courage to reject the "walk like a man, talk like a man, think like a man," mandate. Slowly, society is acknowledging that many women succeed because they are qualified, competent, intelligent, and experienced. Additionally, female leadership characteristics, once a hindrance to success, are being accepted as valuable business skills that are imperative in a changing, diverse, and competitive workforce.

Corporate downsizing in the 1980s and 1990s introduced flatter, rather than hierarchical organizations and, in part, this new structure precipitated a change in attitude toward the female leadership style. During this period *reengineering* became the buzzword and companies needed managers who could inspire and motivate employees, so they turned to women. Supervisory training manuals were rewritten to incorporate collaborative management principles.

The impersonal nature of our society as a result of technology also highlights the need for female leadership. Computers now touch every aspect of our daily lives resulting in customers and employees becoming numbers, passwords, charts, and graphs rather than real people. And it is getting worse, not better. Experts predict that computers will soon be one hundred times more powerful than they are today, and they will virtually take over most of the linear and managerial functions in business. Yet, in this rapidly changing, high-tech world, customers and employees are clamoring for greater personalization. Many employees turn down opportunities with other companies offering more money because they feel a sense of family with their current employer. Customers are more loyal when they feel valued and special—when there is a relationship. Women excel at building relationships, and this skill will be a hot commodity in the new economy.

There is substantial evidence that when women are given the opportunity to be in charge, they are extremely successful. In a 1993 study of senior managers conducted by the Hagberg Consulting Group, female executives outscored their male counterparts in forty-one of forty-seven management criteria, including leadership and problem solving.[1] During an interview on *NBC Nightly News,* Richard

Hagberg said, "What emerged was the picture of women executives as having a more appropriate style of managing in the new millennium. It's a much more team-oriented style."[2]

Companies that are slow to recognize the changing business horizon and continue to clone themselves by building an organization with ranks of managers who look alike and think alike are dinosaurs, soon to follow in the footsteps of their prehistoric ancestors. Building a diverse and inclusive organization is a strategic business imperative, and women entrepreneurs are setting the standards. They are creating a new business paradigm for the new economy. You can capture a glimpse of what future organizations may look like by observing the way women entrepreneurs lead their companies. These women know how use their communication skills to create networks, not hierarchies, within their organizations.

"I think more than anything the difference between men and women is not how we run our businesses, but how we lead. I think women lead more easily as nurturers and builders of talent. We tend to bring out the best the person has to offer, whereas, I think men have more of an autocratic leadership style. With the prevailing corporate wisdom of making people part of the process and engaging all employees, women executives should definitely lead the way in the new decade," said Flori Roberts, founder of Flori Roberts Cosmetics.

"I thought there was something wrong with me because I'm not a hierarchical person. Then I read a book by Sally Helgesen, which talked about the web of inclusion. As a manger I have an open-door policy. I listen to everyone's input. To me, title does not dictate whether or not there is relevance in what you say. I look for skill sense. I work with the approach that I'm putting an idea on the table, and my purpose is to have other people add to it and walk away with a better idea than I started with," explained Vanessa Freytag, president of W-Insight, Inc.

There are new opportunities for women in the new economy. However, although the business world is evolving and adopting a feminine style of leadership, feminine leadership characteristics will not entirely replace traditional management concepts. What will emerge is a blended style that combines collaborative techniques with some of the traditional methods. Exclusive adherence to one type of leadership is shortsighted and will undoubtedly undermine your ability to succeed.

Successful and powerful women selectively choose the strongest, most effective fibers of both styles and weave them together to create a more durable fabric. A blended leadership style allows you to obtain a competitive advantage. You should utilize your natural leadership strengths while analyzing, developing, and fine-tuning those skills that can enhance your overall effectiveness.

It's Okay to Use a Little Feminine Charm

Sometimes being a woman in the business world can have its advantages. Who hasn't occasionally used their feminine wiles to get in the door? There is nothing wrong with that. After all, business is about creating opportunities.

"Years back when I was in sales, there was a type of man who would take calls from a woman, just so [he] could talk to a woman. I had to make sure through the process of developing this prospect that they took me seriously, that they were the decision maker, and not looking to schedule a meeting for anything other than what my intentions were. It was much easier for me as a woman to get an appointment with that kind of man than others. I used the prejudice in the reverse," explained Kim Calero, president of Successful Business Strategies Group.

"You would be surprised, if you hold your ground, how many men would take you seriously and respect you for it. If it took a skirt to get in the door, I would do it. We all know the most difficult part is getting in the door, and then step two is to prove yourself once you are in," she continued.

As Calero says, getting in the door is only half the battle. Good legs and a pretty face won't land you the job or get the business— well, at least not in anyway I care to discuss. Once inside, you must be prepared to dazzle them with competency, knowledge, expertise, and experience. Mediocrity won't work, and you certainly don't have the advantage of the good ole boys' network. You must prove you are better than the best. It is an opportunity to demonstrate that you are a serious business professional.

"The scrap metal business is almost entirely men, and I have to say I used being feminine in my younger days when I was just getting started. I think that's okay. It was wonderful because you have to get in the door to get the job. But nobody does business with you just because you're beautiful or just because you're sexy. They do business with you because you know what you're doing, the other stuff is just extra," said Marsha Serlin, CEO of United Scrap Metal.

According to a survey of more than three hundred executive women conducted by Deborah Swiss, and published in her book *Women Breaking Through: Overcoming the Final 10 Obstacles at Work*, almost 60 percent of the respondents found being female had at one time or another been an advantage in their careers.[3] When you are a woman and do things well, people notice you because you are an anomaly.

"I was working with a man from a very large bank ($88-billion asset-based lending division), and I mentioned to him that he has a lot of women working in his group. And he said he found that women do better in the ABL industry than men. Women can get into a lot of places men can't get into. Plus, they are more detailed in the way their write-ups are done, and they are more dependable. They aren't out on the golf course all the time," said Kay Berry, vice president of KBK Financial.

Personally, having been a former state beauty queen and a runner-up in the Miss America pageant, I managed to "get in the door" when I was job searching because people were curious. They saw the beauty queen image juxtaposed with a strong academic record, and it didn't fit the typical stereotype. Men were and continue to be particularly intrigued by the concept of beauty and brains. Once in the door, however, I had to prove that I was more than a sideshow novelty and get them focused on my credentials.

Some women shun the thought of using a little feminine charm. Perhaps, they see it as copping out, abandoning the sisterhood or something like that. Men and women have differences, and if you can use those differences to create an advantage in your favor—go for it girl. Just make sure you know your stuff.

You Need a Little Chutzpah

"One hears a great deal today about 'the end of hierarchy.'
This is blatant nonsense. In any institution there has to be a
final authority, that is a 'boss'— someone who can make the
final decisions and who can expect them to be obeyed."

—Peter Drucker, Management Challenges for the 21st Century

Organizations are steering away from the command-and-control management style to a more collaborative, team approach. The effectiveness of collaborative management is undisputed. Research has confirmed employees are more productive when they are part of a team where their ideas are valued and their efforts rewarded. Women are good leaders in a collaborative environment. We have the ability to humanize the workplace by tuning into employees as people with lives outside the office. We know how to motivate and encourage others to excel.

While the ability to motivate and build relationships is an important and critical element of leadership, dynamic leadership is broader and more complex. Powerful leadership means, at times, you actually have to step out in front and lead. You must be willing to step beyond the role of a team member and make the final call. That takes confidence and a little chutzpah.

Entrepreneur Flori Roberts notes that some of the top CEOs,

including General Electric's Jack Welch, are autocrats, but they are good ones. "One of the reasons they are so good is their willingness to delegate responsibility and accountability to their managers and allow them to grow as leaders. However, as a business owner, I learned on the job that although you consult, collaborate, consider, and connect with your team, in the end, whether you're male or female, you must make the final decision," she said.

As women, we have a unique opportunity to flex our leadership style between the collaborative and the more authoritarian traditional male style. The test becomes knowing when and how to adapt in the new economy.

To maintain a sense of teamwork and balance with associates in her department, Vanessa Freytag solicits their input, but she acknowledges there are times when not everyone is going to get a vote. "In those situations, I communicate with them up front that something is nonnegotiable. Because I'm usually very open-minded and fair when I say, 'Okay, here's the way it is,' they respect it because they know that in other situations, I ask for their input. I think it's all in how you frame it," she said.

The American Business Women's Association (ABWA) has been conducting leadership training since 1987. According to the executive director Carolyn Elman, "We stress the fact that there are times when a more command and control style is very appropriate and very needed and times when you need to have a collaborative approach. You must focus on the results you're trying to achieve and adapt to the situation."

Do you remember Maslow's Hierarchy of Needs from high school or college? Maslow's hierarchy is a pyramid that begins with the basic creature comforts on the bottom and at the top of the pyramid is self-actualization. Management theorists argue that if you give people a chance to self-actualize, they will be motivated. Sharon Hadary, who studied Maslow's original writings, explained the concept more fully: "What Maslow says is that if you give people a chance to self-actualize, they'll usually get it, but he also said every now and then you've got to hit people over the head with a two-by-four to get their attention. Then, he said, you can create an environment where people can self-actualize. What all this boils down to is that there are times when you do have to use an authoritarian style to get people's attention or to deal with particular situations, but women don't want to make that their preferred or regular style of leadership."

Get out your two-by-four and learn how to swing it. While your employees enjoy the opportunity to be part of the decision-making process, they understand that business needs sometimes require that you be the one to call the shots. Your employees and coworkers will respect you more as a dynamic leader when you demonstrate you have some chutzpah. Don't be a wimp. You must be a powerful leader.

There Are Some People You Just Can't Save

When it comes to personnel issues, one of the biggest pitfalls for women in business is their inability to cut the cord. Because we develop strong relationships in the workplace and are good nurturers, we often fail to discipline employees or make personnel decisions in a timely fashion. We ignore red flags because we are doing our best to salvage each employee—to make things work out.

"Women engage, inspire, give responsibility, and help employees grow. But you have to have some balance in your style because you can keep structures and people in place too long. I've kept people in positions far longer than I should have, but I felt I owed them because they started with me. It ended up being a detriment to my company. Now I've realized you just can't let that happen," explained Flori Roberts.

As part of a matrix team at IBM, Sarah Hudanich saw this firsthand. "They hired a team of managers to launch a new sales initiative. The male managers quickly replaced most of their teams with new folks, or folks they had worked with in the past. The women kept the team intact, and tried to redirect the team to the new direction. Unfortunately, the women managers had a tougher road, and eventually moved on. On the one hand, I feel women are more sensitive to employee morale and seek out loyalties, which is great for the long term. However, I think in certain situations we need to rank the bottom line results piece a little higher," Hudanich explained.

Disciplining or terminating an employee is never easy. It is probably the most difficult issue any business professional has to face—man or woman. I seriously doubt anyone enjoys letting an employee go. I remember how I agonized over terminating a young, single mother weeks before the Christmas holidays even after I caught her stealing from the company. There was no other way to handle the situation because she had been caught red-handed, but it was upsetting nonetheless. However, successful and powerful women know when and how to let go.

"You must examine your motives, and make sure you are doing it for the right reasons, and then you need to handle it in a humane way. You want to think about what you're going to say and be straight about it. You don't want to go blundering through the process because you don't want to leave any room for miscommunication. You don't want the person to walk out and be confused about what just transpired," said professional coach Beverly Berner.

"There was this woman I hired who had good credentials. I thought she knew retail and how to work with people. But after I hired her, she started having incidents with my customers where she'd get angry and smart off to them," explained Ann Ross, founder of The Paper Warehouse chain.

After each customer complaint, Ross would call the employee into her office to discuss the situation. "She'd agree with me, but then it would happen again. Finally, after I had given her chance after chance, we agreed it wasn't working out and we parted ways. The UPS man came in the next day and asked where she was. I told him she wasn't here anymore. And he said 'Well, it's about time.' That was when I knew I had been far too tolerant and patient and that it was really harmful to the store," Ross said.

When you discipline or terminate an employee make certain that you have all the facts straight. Keep your conversation private, and be honest and fair. Remember, there are myriad legal issues involved with disciplining and/or terminating an employee, so make certain that you consult a trained professional before taking any action. Once you know you are within your legal rights, if you can't bring yourself to deliver the bad news personally, consider hiring a human resource manager for your company or rely on a professional from your company's personnel department.

"I can't deliver bad news to anyone. I just try to fix it. I'm much more tolerant than I should be and I find a lot of women are like that. So here I am after twenty plus years in business and I can't get rid of people, and that's costing us about a half a million dollars per year. So I've learned my lesson, and I hired a board of directors to help guide my company to the next level. I also hired a chief operating officer to create a more professionally managed company. We're making lots of good changes," explained Marsha Serlin.

Dealing directly, fairly, and professionally with your employees is a sign of respect. An employee who isn't working out with your company may thrive in another organization. Sometimes personalities and organizational cultures don't click. But most important, the failure to act in a timely fashion can create a total breakdown in your organization because others, including your customers, will loose respect for you. As a powerful leader, that is something you must avoid.

Avoid Being Sabotaged by an Open Door

Unscheduled tasks and personal encounters are not viewed as interruptions by most women. We are multitaskers, and we are good at shifting gears and juggling several projects at the same time. We also like being accessible to others and being seen as caring, involved, helpful, and responsible. Unfortunately, maintaining an unqualified open-door policy can eat up valuable time, be emotionally draining and physically demanding and can seriously impact your overall effectiveness—just ask Sara Hudanich.

"I was brought in as a regional manager, and I had a male counterpart. Our styles were completely different. Mine was nurturing and his was more authoritative. We both had equal successes, except that my style was much more taxing on me personally. I had an open-door policy and people would just come in, shut the door, and want to talk. We'd work through issues, whereas, people would go in his office, the door would remain open most of the time, and they were in and quickly came out. Interestingly, our employee morale numbers were very similar. Mine were a little higher, but not much higher given the amount of time and effort I exerted," said Hudanich.

Open-door policies are good, but you must establish parameters; otherwise, people will take advantage. Learn how to shut the door from time to time so you can focus on your own work.

"The problem with an open-door policy is that I found myself just with so little time to do the other things I needed to do. As one of the few female managers, I was just inundated. People who did not report to me often came to me looking for help. I did have to learn where to draw the line and that was hard for me," explained Vanessa Freytag.

A colleague used to walk into my office with a coffee cup, sit down in a chair across from my desk, and start talking about anything and everything. Initially, I put up with her intrusions until they became so frequent that she was really getting on my nerves. So whenever I saw her walking toward my office, I would grab a file and head for the door. As she approached, I would explain that I was on my way to a meeting, and if she needed to talk with me, she could call and we could schedule a time later. Eventually, she got the hint and her drop-bys ceased.

Be approachable, but lay some ground rules. No one will begrudge you time to get your own work done, in fact, they will probably respect you more. And you will be more successful as a result.

Don't Take It Personally

"I don't know the key to success, but the key to failure is trying to please everybody."

—Bill Cosby

Are you a victim of what talk-show host Oprah Winfrey calls the disease to please? Do you constantly worry about what others will think? If you do, you are not alone. Most women want to be liked—to be popular. Locked in the sophomoric mentally of high school, we all secretly want to be a popular cheerleader, or the prom queen. However, this insatiable quest to be Miss Congeniality creates problems for us professionally.

In business, the fear that someone won't like you can paralyze you, causing you to postpone or avoid making necessary business decisions. It can also inhibit you from taking career-enhancing actions for yourself.

"As women, we are much more caring, and we really worry about how we affect our employees and other people. We want to be liked, that's our big problem. As long as I've been in business, I still take everything personally, and I'd love to get over that," said Marsha Serlin.

To be a dynamic leader, you have to face the facts—not everyone is going to like you. There are some people who aren't going to like you because you remind them of their mother-in-law, or their former wife. Others may dislike you because they are envious of your talents and your success. But success in business is not based on popularity. Successful women recognize the difference between business and friendship. They can make the tough call, and when someone takes exception, they can deal with it without falling apart. "I think that's the key for women sometimes. They don't have to like you, they need to respect you," explained Barbara Dressel, CEO of Automark.

"There will be people that you work well with and others where the differences just can't be resolved. You have to accept that these situations will happen. The important thing is to focus on the best outcome for whatever it is you're trying to achieve and move on," said Barbara Wilkinson, vice president of external affairs at Southwestern Bell.

"I adapted a philosophy early on that the word *bitch* in the business world can be the best backhanded compliment a woman can earn. The term usually means a woman [who] has held her own on the battlefield and that she has earned her stripes. This philosophy has forced me to look at things as purely business and not personal," said Karen Harriman, vice president of marketing and development at a regional health care company.

If you are suffering from the disease to please, get over it. There are some people you'll never be able to please, and there are those who are never going to like you no matter how hard you try. Worrying about what other people think is like shooting yourself in the foot. It is debilitating. So save yourself the aggravation and focus on what is best for you and your business.

Don't Shy away from Confrontation

The majority of women I interviewed for this book said unequivocally they don't like confrontation. Because women take things personally, they have a propensity to shy away from adversarial situations. Many of us go to great lengths to avoid a disagreement, which can actually make the situation worse. How many times have you said, "Oh, it's okay. Don't worry about it. I really don't mind," when you were fuming on the inside?

Very few people truly enjoy conflict. But professional disagreements or altercations can be healthy and productive. When you avoid addressing a problem you have with someone because you don't want to ignite a disagreement, there is the potential for future disaster. Not dealing with the situation leaves you feeling anxious and miserable because you have no place to go with your anger except to internalize it. The longer you put up with the situation, the angrier you become, and your resentment eats away at you like a rapidly growing cancer until it consumes you. When that happens, you risk jeopardizing your professionalism because your bitterness may impact the quality of your work. You might experience stress-related health problems, such as ulcers or migraines, and it is likely that you will take your hostility out on others around you. Eventually, you could explode in an irrational manner, causing you to look like an out-of-control lunatic.

So before you go home and kick the dog, learn how to manage conflict and confront problems head-on to facilitate a timely resolution. Confronting a situation before it gets out of control can actually enhance communication between the parties and circumvent a deteriorating professional relationship.

One of the companies I worked for intentionally fostered an adversarial environment as a methodology for uncovering the best business decision. The CEO pitted his top-level executives against one another, requiring us to argue our positions. This strategy stemmed from a philosophy that the best ideas would emerge through the exercise of debate. You never dared attend one of these meetings unprepared. You needed an arsenal of facts and figures to substantiate your position. And these meetings could get rather heated—definitely not for the thin-skinned. Department heads, division presidents, and senior managers battled it out until ultimately a decision was made. Afterward, everyone left the meeting shaking hands, ready to go to the bar down the street to grab a beer. There were never any hard feelings. For me, it took some getting used to, but I soon learned to appreciate the exercise, and not to fear the confrontation.

One Sunday on *Meet the Press*, I heard author William Bennett describe a rift between then presidential candidate Governor George W. Bush and Congressman Tom Delay as a manly dispute. He said that neither man was going to go off and brood about it. In my opinion, his inference was that if it were a couple of women, they would go off into separate corners and lick their wounds, instead of "taking it like a man."

"Men go into a meeting, they battle it out, and they walk out and everything is okay. Women go into the meeting, battle it out, and we tend to personalize it. So, I try to separate what is a personal issue versus what is a business issue. More women need to learn this if they are going to make it, and it is something I'm still working on," said Catherine Garda Newton, CEO of Bearoness Creations.

Leaders don't permit people to walk all over them. There are times when you have to throw down the gauntlet and say enough is enough. Perhaps, you might even need to do something outrageous.

Soon after Marsha Serlin started her business, one of her best customers, who owed her $3,000, tried to argue that the money wasn't due for a couple of months. Furious and desperately in need of funds, Serlin decided to do something outrageous. While her customer was fumbling through papers to find a document to prove his point, she perched herself on the corner of his desk, lit a cigarette lighter, and proceeded to set the place on fire—literally.

"There was a wastebasket right next to me which had manila folders in it. With my lit cigarette lighter I took the manila folders and one at a time, I set fire to them. Then, I flipped each one over my shoulder. And I kept doing this with folder after folder. People were running in with fire extinguishers. They thought I was crazy. I said, 'Give me a check,' and I got the money," Serlin recalled. "Even after all that, he said he still wanted to do more business with me. I said fine, but I left, went to the bank, cashed the check, then never saw or spoke to him again. I had the courage because I had a family to feed, and I couldn't give up. It gave me the courage to confront this situation and all challenges head on."

Although starting a fire is a bit extreme, Serlin's story makes a good point about not backing down. Don't be guilty of being the one who always gives in or bends over backward to make things work out. You will be perceived as a wimp, not a strong leader. To succeed in business, you must be prepared to face confrontation in a professional, problem-solving manner. Take the emotion out of the situation and deflect personal attacks. Don't be guilty of taking personal potshots, either. Keep it clean and stick to the issues and facts. Then, when it's over, it's over. Shake hands and get on with your life.

Frazzled Isn't a Good Look—Keep Your Emotions in Check

Why is it okay for men to fly off the handle in a fit of rage, but when women do it, they are out of control? You can chalk it up to PMS or an inability to cope, but women get a bad rap if they show their emotions at work. It is another example of a double standard.

Let me tell you about Frank. Frank was a division president at one of the companies I used to work for. Frank had a volatile temper, and would throw a temper tantrum when he was angry. He was aggressive, loud, and childish—a real bully. On occasion, he would call my office about a problem and then start ranting and raving on the telephone. If there were other people in my office, I would hold the receiver away from my ear so that they could hear him screaming at me, and we would all get a good laugh. But it really wasn't funny, and what was most perplexing to me was that management never criticized him for his inappropriate and abusive behavior. They would shrug their shoulders and say, "That's just Frank." Conversely, at one point, I let my anger get out of control with Frank, and the conversation escalated into a heated war of words. The vice president of human resources reprimanded me for not being deferential enough to a division president.

Dynamic leaders exemplify incredible skill when it comes to controlling their emotions. Don't misunderstand me, I don't mean to insinuate they are insensitive or cold, but they maintain their professionalism at all times. The reality is that loosing your cool is unprofessional, regardless of your gender. As a woman climbing to the top, that is not the image you want your associates to have of you. If you are truly stressed out, and you think you might fly off the handle, take a break from the situation. Come back to it when you have calmed down and pulled yourself together.

"Women sometimes let their emotions get in the way of business. We had a horrible client once that we actually had to fire because she would scream and carry on. It just wasn't acceptable," said Iris Salsman, who owns Salsman Lundgren Public Relations.

Beverly Berner, president of the Resource Development Group, coaches women in this area, and she says it is important to take the emotion out of the situation and deal with the facts. "When you see somebody being really emotional and stamping their feet, they're letting the kid take over. Or if you see someone trying to scold and sort of shame you, then they're trying to act like a parent. You need to act like an adult, and deal with the facts. It makes it a whole lot easier to make things happen," she said.

Emotions can well up quickly, and before you know it, you explode. Whatever you do or say in an emotional outrage can't be good. Your emotions impair your judgment, and you will always be the loser. Once the words are out, you can't take them back. Stop and think before you lash out. Hold your breath and count to ten if that is what it takes.

"When I write a memo I think has the potential to be inflammatory, I create it and save if for at least two hours. Then, I read back through it and make sure I've gotten the emotion out of it," explained Catherine Garda Newton.

"When I am angry I must be very careful because I am capable of using very cutting comments or remarks. I've learned to control this type of behavior by writing my thoughts down and working through the problem that caused my anger. This method prepares me to appropriately handle the situation and the person," said Karen Harriman. "I've taken a hundred deep breaths and sometimes it just doesn't help. At that point, I must make a decision to walk away from it, or if

I am in a meeting, to reschedule to another time or day. This approach let's me reclaim my sanity and my leadership," she continued.

Tempers have no place in the business world, nor do tears. But what woman hasn't at some point in her career burst into tears at the office? Tears come naturally to many of us, but you don't want to be labeled a crybaby. When you feel the waterworks creeping up on you, get out of there. Excuse yourself and go to the ladies' room until you have gathered your composure. You don't have to be embarrassed. It is a natural reaction, but men hate it. Candidly, most women feel uncomfortable when you tear up, too.

"I only cry in the office with my door closed [and] on the phone to my mother. You have to do it. You have to channel it however you channel it," said attorney Bonnie Glatzer, partner with the law firm of Thelen, Reid, and Priest.

"In our leadership training we have a whole section about what makes women feel uncomfortable and certainly tears is one of those topics. You obviously see tears more with women, and women want to know what to do about it. You can address it and say, 'I'm feeling pretty emotional right now. I need a couple of minutes, and I'll be right back.' If you can't get over it, explain that this is not a good time for me to talk about this and make an appointment to come back and discuss it later," explained Carolyn Elman, executive director of ABWA.

You Can Negotiate Anything

Successful and powerful women are good negotiators. However, does the thought of negotiating anything make you weak in the knees? Are you afraid that you can't do it? You couldn't be more wrong. Women are born negotiators.

You negotiate every day of your life. You negotiate with your children over whether or not they can sleep over at a friend's house. You negotiate with your friends about where you are going to meet for dinner. You negotiate with the contractor over when he is going to finish the new backyard deck, and how much he is going to charge you for the minor revisions. There are lots of ways to negotiate, and you just don't think of it in those terms. But, most women are pretty darn good at it.

Okay you say, but business negotiations are different than your day-to-day negotiations, right? Wrong. Most likely you perceive business negotiations as hard-hitting, competitive, and tough, and the thought of them scares you. According to the premier book on negotiation, *Getting to Yes* by Roger Fisher and William Ury along with Bruce Patton of the Harvard Negotiation Project, which focuses on principled negotiation, it doesn't have to be that way.

The authors suggest that you look for mutual gains whenever possible, and that where your interests conflict, you should insist that the result be based on some fair standards independent of the will of either side. The method of principled negotiation is hard on the merits, soft on the people. It employs no tricks and no posturing. Principled negtiation shows you how to obtain what you are entitled to and still be decent. It enables you to be fair while protecting you against those who would take advantage of your fairness.

Now, with that definition of negotiation in mind, think about what it means to compromise. A compromise occurs when two people arrive at an agreement that meets with mutual satisfaction. There is nothing intimidating about it, and it utilizes one of your greatest skills as a woman—collaboration.

"A woman's style of collaboration—working it out for the better of the whole can be a very effective method of negotiating," said Sharon Hadary.

"I think the perception is that women are really soft in negotiations, and they don't understand that women can have very concrete goals. The difference is how they reach those goals. It's not about getting everything I can squeeze out of you so you feel poorly walking away. It can be that the compromise you are willing to make, I was prepared to make when I went in. It wasn't something that I actually gave up that was important to me at all. There are a lot of ways to negotiate," explained Vanessa Freytag.

A negotiation is successful when there is a win-win situation. Yet, most men approach negotiations with a competitive strategy— *they* want to win. A negotiation is not about winning and losing. However, men posture themselves to appear aggressive, and they want to score points. That is why they often fail in negotiations.

"I think women—maybe because they're socialized to be hostesses or to be gracious or whatever—don't have a problem making the other side feel like they've gotten all the good points. You can be a very shrewd negotiator by letting the other side think they're getting points, while you're negotiating an excellent agreement for your client," explained attorney Bonnie Glatzer.

For example, when one of the managing partners at Glatzer's firm was a fourth- or fifth-year associate, she participated in a large corporate negotiation with one of the senior partners. "After they had negotiated a number of points with the other side, the client took her aside and said, 'When we go back in, I'm going to have the partner stay out, and I'm going to have you negotiate these next points because they're critical points for us and we're afraid his style is so aggressive that he's killing the deal.' And she successfully completed the negotiation," Glatzer continued.

To prepare for a negotiation, make certain that you have done your homework and that you are well prepared. Always be able to back up your position with substantive facts—emotions don't persuade, facts do. Take time to rehearse before you begin. Practice the way you want to present your case and be organized. Don't fumble through files searching for documentation. Arrange your material so it is always at your fingertips. Anticipate objections, and know going in what your bottom line is and what you are willing to give up. Finally, be open and willing to listen to the other side. Use your facilitative communication skills to your advantage. Ask open-ended questions and encourage your opponent to elaborate. Sometimes you'll find out exactly what it will take to reach an agreement simply by asking the right questions and listening.

Negotiation skills are important for dynamic leaders. The more skilled you become, the more effective you will be.

Notes

1. Anne Thomson, "Women Execs Ready to Reach for Top," *NBC Nightly News*, www.msnbc.com/news/299248.asp, August 10, 1999.
2. Ibid.
3. Taken from a national survey of 325 professional women called "Breaking through the Gender Barriers."

THE POWER OF PLANNING

"Something that is different than when I was first hired is that there are no career paths anymore. You are your own career manager. That's freeing and scary at the same time because there is no cookbook approach—path—anymore."

—Sarah Hudanich, former computer company executive

Taking It One Step at a Time

Where do you want to be five years from now? Ten years from now? Can you answer these questions with a degree of confidence? If you can't, then most likely you are letting events and circumstances control your life. In order to be successful and powerful, you must take responsibility for your success. The worst thing you can do is let your personal business growth and development happen haphazardly. You should establish a lifetime plan of where you want to go. Then, make decisions that advance you toward your goals, one step at a time.

"Life throws you a whole bunch of curveballs, and if you don't have a plan, there's really nothing to hold on to," explained Sarah Hudanich.

According to Eric Segal, the chief operating officer (COO) of Kenzer Corporation, career planning is no different from retirement planning. The more thought you put into it, the more likely that you will reach your eventual goal. "It means you'll be better equipped to analyze every roadblock, every crossroad, every opportunity that comes your way within the business world. I think that developing a strategic plan for your individual career is as critical as any other business planning or personal planning you do," he commented.

Even if you are content in your current position, good career strategists advise you to never stop looking around. Consider it a passive job search. Keep your eyes and ears open and keep your resume current. You want to be poised to identify and seize advancement opportunities when they come your way.

Continuous networking is important because it forces you to constantly reevaluate your skills and stay abreast of current trends. Plus, it ensures that when it comes time to do a job search you won't be scrambling. In today's competitive market, it is often who you know, not what you know, that is most important.

Create a personal mission statement, and put it in writing. There is something powerful about seeing the words on paper. Your mission statement should identify your strengths, your passion, your core beliefs and values, and what direction you want your life to take. In other words, your mission statement should reflect your vision for the future, so think big and be brutally honest with yourself.

Once you have created your mission statement, begin developing strategies to get you there. Your strategies should be flexible, not written in concrete. Keep an open mind when considering new opportunities. However, any career move should be juxtaposed with your personal mission statement to make certain that it is in sync with your values and goals.

It takes discipline to create a personal strategic plan, but without a plan it is impossible to know where you are going or if and when you have achieved your goals. Even with a plan, it is easy to get sidetracked. This often occurs when the realities of life come crashing down around you, tempting you to do something because you think it's what you should do, rather than what you really want to do.

Before I started writing this book, I was offered a senior-level position with an international company. For weeks, I wrestled with whether or not to accept the job. My husband had recently lost his job, and it seemed more practical to accept a "real" job with a regular paycheck than to strike out on my own. Then, I was talking to one of my dear friends, Juanita Weaver, who said, "I don't hear any excitement in your voice when you talk about this great job, but your eyes light up with you talk about the book. Maybe that should tell you something." Weaver sensed that I was on the brink of compromising my personal vision and plan because it was the "right" thing to do, and fortunately she cared enough to point it out to me. So many of us ignore our personal desires to conform to what we think is expected of us. That is why your mission statement and career plan is important. It is the road map that can keep you on track and help you get to where you want to go.

Wow Them

Perhaps you are one of those people who gets personal satisfaction out of a job well done. Maybe you sincerely believe that if you work hard and produce a quality product, the rewards and recognition will come. Unfortunately, things don't work that way.

Talent and brilliance alone won't get you to the top. You need to launch a personal marketing campaign for yourself. The goal is to "wow" them.

Women aren't good at tooting their own horns, and like many other issues discussed in this book, it is because we are taught that good girls don't brag. While boys grow up vying for the limelight and learning to one-up each other, girls are taught to share the glory. We are not supposed to be the center of attention. Therefore, in business, we sadly watch as we are passed by time and time again for promotions, high-visibility assignments, committee chairs, and so on because we don't draw attention to our accomplishments.

"There was a woman I used to work with who was always tooting her own horn, and I didn't like it. Then, one day I realized that, nonetheless, I was impressed with her track record. Subsequently, I realized you really have to do your own PR work. For a lot of women, including myself, that's hard. But you really do have to do that if you want people to understand what your contributions are," said Juanita Weaver, a creativity consultant.

"Nobody knows you better than you. There's nothing wrong with letting your manager or others know about your successes. But as women, not only do we fail to draw attention to our accomplishments, but we tend to downplay them," said Sharon Hadary.

Self-promotion can be accomplished in an artful and tasteful manner. You don't want to appear too opportunistic, nor do you want to become a legend in your own mind. The best advice is to watch and learn from others.

Make Certain the Right People Know What You Are Doing

Does your boss's boss know what a great job you are doing? Does your sales contact keep his or her supervisors apprised of your company's performance record? Will anyone be aware of your accomplishments if your supervisor or your company contact leaves or gets promoted? If you can't answer yes to these questions with confidence, then you are not doing a good job of marketing yourself. You need an action plan.

"What I try to do personally is document what I do, and let people know about it. You have to recognize that it's okay to say you're good at something, and by documenting things you've done you can show them on paper," said Catherine Garda Newton, a former IBM executive. "I also regularly update my resume because it forces me to look back at what I've done and it keeps it firmly in my mind. I can also evaluate better whether I'm moving forward toward where I want to go."

Look for Opportunities to Tell Your Story

If your company has staff meetings, always be prepared to highlight your results. Utilize internal memos and weekly or monthly progress reports as a method of keeping associates informed of your accomplishments. Use opportunities to remind your customers of your performance record. Rather than bragging, you'll appear competent and professional for keeping everyone informed.

Be Generous with the Praise of Others

Make certain your business associates, employees, or team members receive recognition for a job well done. When you are quick to sincerely praise the good work of others and allow them to bask in the limelight, they will readily do the same for you. You won't have to say a thing about yourself because your associates will enthusiastically carry your banner.

Use External Sources

Enhance your credibility and stature by writing an article for a trade journal or a business publication. Establish yourself as a resource with the media—someone they can call when they need an authority to quote. Send out news releases announcing your business successes. Share published articles with your business associates and customers. Of course, always make certain you have permission to copy printed materials so you don't infringe on a publication's copyright.

Write a Dazzling Bio

Create a personal bio that wows them. If you are not a good writer, hire someone who can do it for you. Even though I have been a marketing professional for more than twenty years, I hire marketing professionals to write for me. These professionals have the objectivity to make me sound great. If you choose to do it yourself, make certain that you highlight your achievements and experience as well as any awards or special recognition you may have received. The goal is to look like the superstar you are.

There is a delicate balance when it comes to self-promotion, and you don't want to be guilty of overkill. But when used appropriately, a personal marketing campaign can create magic for you and help you get to where you want to go. Marketing yourself is like marketing your business—if no one knows about your product, who will buy it?

Taking Risk Is Part of the Game—Go for It

"You can only become a winner if you are willing to walk over the edge."
—Ronald E. McNair, astronaut

Research shows that men are more willing to take risks than are women. However, I disagree with the research findings. Most successful women have taken significant risks at some point in their careers to get to the top. They have made career changes. They have moved to new cities and countries. They have accepted tough assignments, and they have started multimillion-dollar enterprises on a shoestring budget. Dynamic, intelligent women who have a vision understand that life is not a dress rehearsal, and to make the most of it; you've got to stick your neck out once in a while and go for it.

"It's easy to stagnate, stay in that comfortable secure zone, rather than [take] those risks. Risk challenges us to be the best we can be, and in those 'risky' situations often you have no other choice but to be at your best. Taking those risks gives you an opportunity to see inside yourself and see what you are really all about. It's a fabulous experience, and the rewards received are both personal and professional, regardless of whether you reach your goal or not," stated Kim Calero, president of Successful Business Strategies Group.

People who are afraid of taking risks rarely enjoy the sweet success of winning. But taking a risk does not mean taking a blind leap of faith. You should carefully analyze the pros and cons of a situation before you jump.

"I'd describe myself as a calculated risk taker. I wouldn't ever want to cause harm to anyone that I love or care about, or bring us to financial ruin because of a haphazardly taken chance. So, I try to sort of play chess. I think about the 'what ifs,' the worst-case scenarios before I do anything so I am prepared for my options," explained Linda Jacobsen, president of Global Vision Strategies.

Some women, particularly those with an entrepreneurial bent, are natural risk takers. The thrill of living on the edge excites and energizes them. The more confident you are with your own abilities, the less concerned you are about taking a chance because you know you can land on your feet.

A fear of failure is what prevents most women from taking risks. They dwell on the negatives and weigh themselves down with a "what if it doesn't work out" attitude. So what if it doesn't work out? Is the world suddenly going to come to an end?

Margaret McEntire decided to take a risk and start a business selling bouquets made out of candy. In her first year, she lost nearly $50,000 and was on the verge of losing the family home. At that point most people would have given up, but Margaret remained focused on the positive. One night as she sat in her kitchen burning the midnight oil, her son came in, sat down next her, and asked her if she was afraid. McEntire said, "Son, the only thing you have to fear is fear itself, and I'm not afraid because winners never quit and quitters never win. And I'm not a quitter."

McEntire's willingness to take a gamble, along with her commitment and perseverance, paid off. Today, there are 440 Candy Bouquet franchises in forty-eight states and thirty-two countries. But if she hadn't risked everything and stared disaster boldly in the face, she might still be asking, "What if?"

Wisdom comes from failure. Some of the most talented and successful people in the world have had miserable failures. We all learn from our mistakes. Trust me, your world won't come to an end if you don't succeed the first time you try something new. Remember when you were learning to ride a bicycle. Did you get on and peddle down the street the first time? I doubt it. Most likely you had a few falls with skinned knees and scraped elbows, but you got back up and tried again until finally you were peddling like a pro. In business if you take a risk and try new things, you'll have a few scraped knees along the way, but that is what it takes to succeed.

"I tell my kids, the difference between the great and the near great is not ability. The difference is the great know how to make a mistake and pick up and go right back after it. You have to take the protective armor off, and realize it's okay if you fail," said Ellen Sherberg, publisher of the *St. Louis Business Journal.*

"Who cares if somebody calls me stupid or I don't get the business," said Marsha Serlin, CEO of United Scrap Metal. "But women have been brought up to play it safe and not take risks. That's probably why a lot of women haven't gone into their own businesses. They have great ideas, but then they spend the rest of their lives saying, 'I wish I did,' or 'If I would have done this.' I can never be sorry about missed opportunities because I've certainly taken chances."

"I think it's worse not to try. I think a life of regret would be much more painful than trying something wonderful and failing at it," said Jane Applegate, CEO and founder of SBTV.com.

When it comes to risk taking, Barb Gilman, a former investment representative with Edward Jones who became a partner in the firm, is one of the gutsiest women I know. When her youngest child neared high school graduation, Gilman decided to completely change her life. She sold a successful real-estate brokerage business in Manhattan, Kansas, left her friends and family and moved to a relatively small town in Texas to open an Edward Jones investment office. Even though her friends thought she had totally lost it, once she made her decision she never looked back.

"I totally removed the word fail from my vocabulary. It's never been a strong word in my vocabulary, but it [became] nonexistent. After that, nothing could stop me. I wasn't going to let anything get in my way. It ended up being the most challenging and fun period of my life. Everybody I met for the first time was a potential customer, friend, you know, it was neat. It's a matter of attitude," Gilman explained.

The next time an opportunity comes your way that poses an element of risk, don't shy away from it. Remember, life is not a dress rehearsal, and this may be your once-in-a-lifetime opportunity.

Power Comes from a Positive Attitude

"Failure is, in a sense, the highway to success, inasmuch as every discovery of what is false leads us to seek earnestly after what is true."

—John Keats, author

As you can see from the previous examples, women who are wildly successful are not only willing to take risks but are resilient and persistent. They can make a mistake or get a bad break and bounce right back. That is where real power comes from. It comes not from taking charge of your life by not allowing circumstances to control you, but from taking control of the circumstances themselves. When things happen to you that are not ideal, you have two choices: You can dwell on the past and the negatives or your can move on and focus on the future. *It's your attitude that dictates your success.*

For about five years, I have taught a women's entrepreneurial training course at a local college. The class comprises a diverse group of about forty women. On the first day of class, I ask each of the women to introduce themselves and to share a little bit about their personal backgrounds. Semester after semester, I hear amazing stories of women who have faced adversity, and who have bounced back ready to tackle new challenges. Based purely on anecdotal observations, I sincerely believe that women are stronger and more resilient than men are. Regardless of gender, however, the true test becomes not so much in what happens to you, but your perception of how what happens affects your life.

"I am not tolerant of victims—somebody who takes on the mantle of a victim. Life is full of choices. We all stand accountable for the choices we make, and I've always been accountable for my own actions, both personally and professionally," stated Barb Gilman.

Things always happen for a reason. That may sound trite, but it's true. Sometimes it is difficult to comprehend when a failure occurs, but even our biggest failures build character and strength. In the movie *The Sound of Music*, when Maria realizes that she is in love with the captain, and he with her, she says to him: "When God shuts a door, somewhere he opens a window." There is always an open window. Your responsibility is to find it. Winning is great, but nobody wins all the time. Maintain a positive outlook on life and the rewards will come your way.

Moving Onward and Upward

Leaving your current job, selling your business, or changing your life's direction creates anxiety and stress. However, regardless of how stressful it may be, you should never be complacent. Reaching your professional goals means making timely business and career decisions, and sometimes you may have to move out in order to move up.

A native of Boston, Iris Salsman graduated from Emerson College with majors in speech and communication disorders and

English. Marriage lured her away from the East Coast to the Midwest where, after her son was born, she decided to take a part-time job as director of volunteers for a not-for-profit agency. Although she was extremely overqualified for the position, Salsman was determined that it was the right choice at the time.

"The job worked well with my son's schedule. But what I really wanted to do was write and use my creativity. After I had been there a while, the agency needed some help in the communications department. They asked me if I'd be interested, and of course, I said yes because I'd be able to write. They were impressed with me, and told me I was better than the people they had on staff," Salsman explained.

Quickly, Salsman was promoted to the position of assistant director of communications. Then, the department director resigned, and the agency began the hunt for a replacement. Although she was qualified for the director's position, Salsman was told not to apply because the agency wanted a man for the job. So she was passed up for the top spot, and a man was hired instead.

"They hired this young guy, younger than me, and he didn't know much or have much experience. But I decided to stay on because I wanted to make a few more contacts," Salsman said. "But I ended up staying for a year, and I grew increasingly resentful because I was doing so much more than he was. They kept trying to make me feel better by giving me extra vacation, more money, and all that, but they didn't understand that wasn't the issue. I should have seen the handwriting on the wall earlier. Eventually I quit and started my own company. It was the best decision I ever made. If only I had done it sooner."

According to Beverly Berner, president of The Resource Development Group, "Women, I think hang on because you start to think that there is something really wrong with you that for some reason this job isn't working anymore. It happened to me in advertising. I had a great job, with a big office, and I was traveling to fabulous places, dealing with the bigwigs, but I was miserable. I thought there has to be some kind of fatal flaw with me. The best thing that ever happened to me is that I lost my job."

Jane Applegate uprooted her family and moved from Los Angeles to New York for the opportunity of a lifetime. Hired by the chairman of the board of a major media company, Applegate found herself thrust upon an unhappy and unimpressed female supervisor. "As much as I tried to make the relationship work, it was doomed to fail. Yet, every time I went back to the chairman who had hired me, he would give me more money, and ask me to give it another few months. That went on for two years. The money helped until my health failed. The day I resigned was one of the happiest days in my life because I got my freedom back, and I got my health back," remembered Applegate.

There are so many opportunities for women today. When your career is on the road to nowhere, don't hang in there hoping it will get better. Don't blame yourself or desperately search for tidbits of encouragement to justify your decision to stay. You will be building your career on false hope and undermining your self-esteem. Once you have seen the writing on the wall, every day that you postpone your decision to move on is a wasted day on your road to your success.

"The worst thing you can do is end up jumping for the wrong reasons. But if you are in a situation where you believe your company is not paying attention to what you are doing, and you are unfairly locked in your growth potential, begin to look for a company that is going to give you the opportunity to grow. I think there are enough opportunities out there for quality people no matter what your gender is or no matter what your diversity is. But there are companies out there that believe if you are not a male, you do not have a chance to grow. So leave," advised Eric Segal.

Be Open to Lateral or Interindustry Moves

" I think it's very important to take advantage of as many different job opportunities and assignments in a variety of disciplines as you progress, both laterally and upwardly in a company. It's important to get different perspectives from different areas of the business in order to understand how they all contribute to the overall performance of the corporation. And, that has been a part of my career that I have found to be continually stimulating and challenging," said Barbara Wilkinson, vice president of external affairs at Southwestern Bell.

Some of your best career moves may not be straight up. You should search for opportunities that broaden your skill level, industry knowledge, or organizational knowledge. Think of it in terms of packaging. The more varied your skills and knowledge base, the more attractive your overall package becomes because you've added those extra bells and whistles. Furthermore, diversity in experience enhances your ability to creatively solve problems.

Be careful, however, if you are considering a lateral move based purely on money as opposed to career enhancement. "I think making a move for money is like leaving your husband or leaving your wife for another women or man. You don't leave because someone is giving you a couple of dollars more even if you're really not getting what you want out of your current relationship. And, therefore, if you're going to choose another relationship or another company, do it out of knowledge, not just for a couple of dollars. But if after doing a complete evaluation of the company offering an opportunity and it checks out to be the right organization—go for it. You have people looking for additional exposure, therefore, they want to get in with a better company which has a better track record and better opportunity to grow. You want to look at your career and will this move eventually lead you to whatever you want to be. Sometimes the road is not paved in gold, it's a solid steel stepladder," explained Eric Segal.

Ellen Turner, who is senior vice president of sales and marketing at Kinko's, used interindustry moves to broaden her experience. She moved from packaged goods to soft drinks then into retail, media, and technology. In an interview with *Executive Female* magazine, she said her career centered on learning and pushing for more responsibilities as well as taking on challenges and building her skill set.[1]

Before you make any career move, do your homework. Learn as much as you can about the new company's culture, or if it is an intracompany move, get the scoop on the person for whom you will be working. Talk to other employees to see if they are happy, motivated, and challenged. No one works in a vacuum so you should examine all the elements.

Before Vanessa Freytag, a former director of Bank One, accepts a new job, she always looks at the people whom she would potentially work for. "I looked for open-mindedness to a degree. A manager doesn't have to be like me, but I know I won't do well under a dictatorial management style, so I don't go there. The second thing is, I like working for people who are a lot smarter than I am because I want to learn something. If I'm not learning, then I'm bored. And finally, it's important to me to work for somebody who is perceived as a leader," she said.

"I have refused positions in organizations where there were four executive positions open in the last six months and none were filled by a minority or a woman. I said, 'Help me understand why I should believe that there's going to be recognition given and value given for my skills and contributions,'" explained Catherine Garda Newton.

Finally, don't limit yourself geographically. Many more opportunities will open up for you if you are willing to relocate. A recent survey conducted by Runzheimer International of human resource professionals at global companies noted that 70 percent expect to send more women abroad in the next five years.[2]

"Businesses are spread all over today. Even the financial institutions are all over the country—all over the world. And having the ability to be available to go anyplace is a plus factor. If you are living in Charlotte, North Carolina, and you work for First Carolina Bank or whatever the number one bank is down there, and you determine you can't leave Charlotte, then how many career opportunities are there going to be from that?" explained Eric Segal.

Too many career jumps can be detrimental, however. A resume punctuated with frequent job changes every year or two, no matter what your justification, does not bode well. Carefully analyze the benefits of a new opportunity and proceed cautiously.

Notes

1. Gail Gabriel, "Setting No Limits. Kinko's Executive Ellen Turner Sets Her Mind on Leadership," *Executive Female*, www.nafe.com/ef/f9/cover.html, August 18, 1999.
2. Anne Fisher, "Ask Annie Career Advice," *Fortune*, vol. 135, no. 12, July 5, 1999.

THE POWER OF A TURBOCHARGED CAREER

Mentors Can Turbocharge Your Success

Whether you are an entrepreneur or an employee, finding a mentor is one way to put your professional career on the fast track to success. Mentors share their wisdom, advice, and counsel to help you avoid making costly mistakes. It is rare to find a successful woman who hasn't had at least one mentor during her journey to the top.

"There was a partner at a law firm where I worked that would sit in my office and talk to me about the types of work I needed to do—what types of experiences I needed to have and where I needed to put my efforts. Then, there were others who would advise me to do a project for a particular client with a specific partner so that my work would get more visibility. That helped a lot, particularly in a law firm setting," said Bonnie Glatzer, a partner with the law firm of Thelen, Reid, and Preist.

Mentors come in all shapes and sizes. It doesn't matter if they work for a different company or even in a different industry. Syndicated newspaper columnist and author and CEO of SBTV.com Jane Applegate said that she never had a mentor in her own field. "I've had people in totally different areas of business. One was a very high-level government person and another was a financial person. But I think that's good because my mentors in life are informal coaches. They don't know my business, but they have a much more objective view," she explained.

Don't assume that your mentor must be a woman. One of my best mentors was a man, and that is true for many successful women. In an "Ask Annie" column in *Fortune* magazine, a reader made this observation: "If gender is a criterion [that] she's using for selecting a mentor, she doesn't grasp the mentor concept. A mentor should be someone of either sex whom she aspires to be like in five or ten years. I may be 'one of the guys,' but two of my most influential mentors have been women."

How to Find a Mentor

Because companies are beginning to recognize the importance of mentoring, many major corporations offer formalized mentoring programs. Additionally, professional organizations and women's groups can often pair you up with a mentor.

"We estimate there are probably 50 percent of all the women's Jorganizations that have formal mentoring programs. Mentoring has never been more important," said Edie Fraser, president of the Business Women's Network.

For the most part, arranged mentoring relationships are similar to arranged marriages, generally they aren't very successful. The most successful mentoring relationships seem to evolve naturally. However, you can be more proactive and ask someone you admire to be your mentor.

Most people are flattered when you ask them to mentor you. It is a real compliment. After all, don't we all love to give advice? Even the busiest and most successful people are usually willing to share some time with you. However, make certain that you are prepared to explain why you selected him or her to be your mentor, what your expectations are from the mentoring relationship, and be cautious about the amount of time you expect. Also, make certain that your mentor shares your same values and beliefs.

"The problem is [that] people sometimes ask too much of their mentors. You can't expect to have lunch every Thursday for the rest of your life. That frightens people off," said Jane Applegate. "I usually tell people up front, I don't have the time to be their long-term, full-time mentor, but I'm happy to speak to them occasionally. I think the less you ask of someone, the more you're apt to get some of their time. So if you don't fall all over the person and make unreasonable demands for time, you have a much better chance of getting their attention," she explained.

"Unfortunately, we all are experiencing more and more demands on our time. But I try to manage my calendar so that I can stay involved, particularly in mentoring. That's one of the best ways I can offer the benefit of my experience to other women coming up in the company," said Barbara Wilkinson, vice president of external affairs at Southwestern Bell.

Don't expect your mentor to hold your hand and tell you every step to take. Most likely, your mentor will challenge you to define your own personal strategy. Your mentor will expect you to work hard and to be accountable for your results.

"If people talk to me and want some of my time and assistance, I'm very good with that. But I ask them to tell me where they want to be in five or ten years, then I tell them to develop a strategy and plan to get there. No one can do it for you. If I just give them a solution, that doesn't really help them," said Marsha Serlin, CEO of United Scrap Metal.

Because effective mentoring relationships need to have guidelines and parameters, many professional organizations provide training on how to be a good mentor.

"In our ABWA training, we explain what a mentor is and what it's not. I don't know if it's true of men or not, but women, if you're not careful, can cross over into mothering as opposed to mentoring. So we do some work on that," explained Carolyn Elman, executive director of the American Business Women's Association. "We also do some work on really outlining and putting some structure to the mentoring relationship. There is an expected end to it. There should be checkpoints where you make a conscious decision of whether or not to continue."

Overwhelmingly, successful women are generous and sincere in their desire to mentor other women. They view it as an important responsibility, and as a way of helping to ensure greater opportunities for future generations. My philosophy is that what goes around comes around. If you are willing to give of yourself, it will come back to you a million times over.

"Successful people are the most generous of spirit. I've dealt with some very famous, high-level people who have given me their time and not asked for anything in return. They are my role models. I think nobody is that busy or self-important that they can't spend a few minutes with someone. It's always paid off for me," said Jane Applegate.

"Look, I climbed a lot of mountains to get where I am today," said Susan Grode, partner at the Los Angeles law firm of Katten, Muchin & Zavis. "Why should some young woman have to climb those same mountains if she can learn from me instead.[1]

Ask for What You Want

I remember my mother taking me to her friend's home for a visit when I was a little girl. The woman had just taken a batch of chocolate chip cookies from the oven, which were my favorite type, and the aroma of freshly baked cookies filled the air. Shyly, I asked if I could have a cookie. Embarrassed, my mother apologized to her friend and scolded me. She explained that it is not polite to ask for something; you must wait until it is offered. In business, if you don't ask for it, you'll never get it.

"Men seem to be more aggressive in asking for what they want in terms of their career. They will come in and they will say, 'I want to take a plaintiff's deposition because I haven't done that yet.' They pay careful attention to their career strategy. Now, I don't mean to overgeneralize. There are some women who are comfortable with this, but I think a lot of the time the women lawyers are too accommodating. They do their work and if they are dissatisfied with how things are developing, they really don't tell you," said Bonnie Glatzer.

No one wants to be seen as a troublemaker, but you don't want to be a pushover either. Passive management of your business or your career will get you nowhere fast. You must take a proactive approach and ask for what you want, and what you deserve.

While I was working my way up the corporate ladder at ITT, I attended night law school. The company had a tuition reimbursement program, but I was told that a law degree did not qualify for the program. Law school was considered preparation for a career change rather than a career enhancement program. Without any argument, I accepted that answer, and paid for my own way.

About a year after I graduated, I learned that a male manager, several levels below me, was enrolled in night law school, and the company was paying his tuition. I was livid and demanded to know why he was receiving a significant company benefit that I had been denied. No one could give me a good answer, so I wrote a formal complaint letter to the CEO asking for full reimbursement. After several rounds of negotiations with the human resources department, the company reversed its decision and reluctantly reimbursed me for my tuition. It was the fair and equitable thing for the company to do, but it never would have happened if I hadn't been willing to ask for it.

"I make good money with the company I work for now, and I like what I am doing. But the company recently hired several men in another market who are making more money than I do. They also gave them the senior vice president titles, whereas I'm still a vice president. I know I am a valuable asset to a company now, but I realize I'm going to have to ask for the title, if I'm going to get it," said Kay Berry, vice president of KBK Financial.

Don't be afraid to let people know what your professional aspirations are, and don't be afraid to ask for the world. The worst that can happen is that you will be told no.

For more information on mentoring relationships see *Learning from Other Women: How to Benefit from the Knowledge, Wisdom, and Experience of Female Mentors* by Carolyn S. Duff (AMACOM).

Hire a Professional Coach

Coaching bridges the gap from where you are today to where you want to go. A professional coach, unlike a mentor, utilizes professional assessments to help you identify critical information about yourself. These assessments allow you to focus on your goals, life skills, and communication skills. Your coach meets with you to find out what is going on in your mind—what is not working, and what you would like to see happen. According to Beverly Berner, who works with myriad clients as a professional coach, it is about developing a deeper understanding of where your magic is—your gifts and your abilities.

"It's having a confidante by your side co-thinking and co-strategizing about what results you want to achieve. What kinds of obstacles do we see, and how can we work around them or who can you ask. Most people have the answer. A coach can help find them easier, faster and with less pain," Berner explained.

A professional coach begins with the fundamentals of attacking your negative belief systems. What factors are precluding you from reaching your true heart's desire and producing the results you want to produce? A coach can be more objective in evaluating your situation. A coach also helps you tap into your creative realm.

"I work with people [by] actually returning them back to the feelings and the way they viewed life more from a childlike point of view. You know, before the world started beating them down. I actually have them articulate and express what that world looked like and it seems to open up whole new vistas and points of view for people," said Laura Finestone, founder and president of VIA Associates (Vision in Action). "For me there were really strong memories of walking up the road by myself when I was four years old chasing butterflies, and along with that came a sense of freedom. As people start to articulate that, they start acting from that pure place again. They also, as a matter of course, start getting more creative," Finestone continued.

Generally, when you work with a coach you will set objectives for yourself, and you will schedule weekly updates. Because you report in regularly, you stay focused on your objectives.

"I work with people on what are the self-sabotaging mechanisms that they have that keep them winding up in the same place. I focus on: this is who you say you want to be, this is what you say you want to do, this is what you say you're committed to, now what's added or what's missing that causes you to keep having these kind of results. The people who work with me get way more than they bargain for. I've had clients produce amazing breakthroughs in not only their income, but also in their personal growth," explained Finestone.

There are thousands of professional coaches listed on the Internet today, but the best way to find a really good one is by word of mouth. Find out whom your friends and business associates would recommend. Be sure to inquire about the coach's experience and what kinds of results they have produced. Then, shop around.

"Make sure, [just as] if you were interviewing a therapist, that the relationship feels right when you're talking to somebody. Ask about their background and training. Do they come from a psychological background or are they from a business background? It's a question of being responsible, and interviewing and telling the coach this is what I want to produce. Talk to references," said Finestone.

Keep in mind that coaches are not therapists. So be careful you don't confuse the two and expect your professional coach to help you work through pent-up emotional issues. That is not what they are there for.

"I had a meltdown a few years ago because I broke up with my boyfriend and my cat died and all the rest of it and you better believe I was in with a therapist. A coach wouldn't have been the right thing," said Finestone.

Professional coaches can spur you on to greater success. In fact, Beverly Berner is so committed to the process that she herself has a professional coach. "I think all good coaches have coaches. I find that it helps me get over the fear of a lot of things and reinforces my strengths," she said.

Watch out for the Threatened Woman

"The woman is hard upon the woman."

—Alfred Lord Tennyson, poet

"Some women aren't smart enough to say I've got a good person here. She'll make me shine, and I'll make her shine. They are too insecure with their own knowledge," said Barbara Dressel, CEO of Automark.

Although it is perplexing, disheartening, and yet true, some women in business can be manipulative and back stabbing with other women. Fueled by a lack of self-esteem, these women seem to have a survival-of-the-fittest attitude. However, these women can often be chameleonlike, chumming up to you like your best friend, while secretly sabotaging your career. They can be treacherous opponents in the business world.

I joined the marketing department of a growing midsize company after heading the marketing department of an international asset-based lending company with nearly $30 billion in revenue. The position I took at the new company was far below my experience level, but I didn't need the money, and I was excited about the prospect of helping grow the business. I perceived there was opportunity within this burgeoning organization, and I felt my experience would allow me to quickly rise to the top.

I couldn't have been more wrong. The woman partner who headed my area made certain that I had absolutely no visibility. The longer I was there, the worse it got. She limited her interactions with me and treated me like one of the young associates fresh out of college. Fed up, I tendered my resignation, but in doing so I requested a personal meeting with the managing partner. During the meeting, the managing partner said he was sorry I hadn't been given an opportunity, but he summed it up as a personality conflict—in other words, a catfight. His read on the situation was that I had obviously and understandably threatened this woman. The tragic part of this whole incident is the fact the company lost a talented employee, and this woman lost the opportunity for a good friend and ally.

A threatened woman spells disaster when she is your boss. In an April 14, 1999, "Ask Annie" column in *Fortune* magazine, the columnist suggested that women bosses who are manipulative or hard on other females are the exception rather than the rule. She opined that perhaps women load up their female bosses with too many unrealistic expectations. That column generated 266 letters of which 200 indicated this particular columnist didn't have a clue what was happening in the real world. One reader wrote, "Women bosses tend to be catty, jealous, and bitchy—not just some of them, but the vast majority." Many of the women who responded to the article who had bad women bosses found it so difficult that they left corporate America and started their own businesses.

"I've had more competition problems with women than with men. Some men tend not to take women seriously, so they have less of a sense of competition with them. Women get very competitive and jealous and tend to be less straightforward," said Laura Finestone.

Upon handing in her resignation to her department supervisor at the college where she taught, Linda Jacobsen received a cold response that she had not anticipated. Her supervisor, who was a woman, admitted she wasn't sorry to see Jacobsen leave because she had felt forced to compete with Jacobsen during her tenure at the school.

"I looked at her and said, 'Couldn't you just be happy that you had someone in your department whose class was always filled, whose students were always happy to be with her, and whose students excelled?' And she looked at me and she said, 'No, I can't,'" Jacobsen remembered.

"Throughout my education and certain jobs I worked in, excellence was not rewarded. It was seen as threatening. And even now I see other women in organizations and things that I belong to, you can tell which women are threatened by your competence. Instead of rejoicing—'Here's a capable person with an open heart, let's put her to work'—they can throw knives. I think this is one of the things that still undermines women as a gender," explained Jacobsen.

If you happen to be an attractive, intelligent, and talented woman you make an even greater target for the threatened woman. Although being beautiful can give you an edge in some circumstances, when it comes to dealing with an insecure female, watch out.

"Women just don't know how to deal with other women, especially attractive ones. Women who are my peers are very standoffish with me. When I first started in the business, the women purchasing agents wouldn't give me the time of day. I believe there was resentment. It was an attitude that says that I'm just as good or better than you, and I'm going to show you by not giving you the business," said Marsha Serlin. "We can all achieve more if we're aligned, but for some reason women feel better about themselves when they talk about another woman. I don't get it."

When you run into a threatened women, keep your distance and don't waste your time on her. In most cases, you will not be able to change her attitude toward you, and her insecurity is not your problem. Whatever you do, don't be lulled into a false sense of security with her. Keep your eyes open, because the threatened woman is often skilled at hiding her true personality.

Fortunately, most successful women who are confident and comfortable with themselves are not threatened by other women. In fact, it is quite the opposite. They are gracious, warm, helpful, encouraging, and supportive. That is why I love working with other women.

Keep in mind, when one of us succeeds, it is a success for all of us. We need to work together, not against each other. Rejoice in each other's successes because each individual's success lights the way for a brighter future for all of us.

Technology—The Gender Equalizer

In 1977, Ken Olsen, founder of Digital Equipment Corporation, said that there is no reason why anyone would want a computer in their home.[2] I wonder what he might think today. Web surfing has a good chance of becoming more popular than watching television. Children, as well as adults, sit for hours in front of computer screens. Americans are smitten with cyberspace.

Technology is revolutionizing every aspect of our daily lives— from the way we do business to the way we communicate with our friends. We have gone from the primitive printing press to the information superhighway, and it goes without saying—if you aren't cruising down that highway, you're going to be left in the dust.

For years, many women were technophobes. Computers were for geeks with thick glasses and pocket protectors who could manipulate the intricate technolanguage required to understand a computer program. Now, anyone can easily breeze through the user-friendly software programs.

"Five or six years ago, women were 9 percent of Internet users, and today, we have surpassed 50 percent. We were just a little slower to catch on. Technology is changing our lives," said Edie Fraser.

Technology levels the playing field for women in a number of ways. First, the Internet offers an opportunity for people to communicate with each other with fewer prejudices and misunderstandings than ever before. It is virtually gender blind, at least when you are dealing in a professional mode, and it is more of a merit-based system where your ideas are important, not your physical characteristics.

"I've done a lot of work with the disabled community, and over the past few years I've seen how it has changed one minority group, and I think we're seeing it change women in a lot of the same ways, and it does level the playing field. All of a sudden, you're not looked at as a white woman in a wheelchair or a black man who can't see. All of a sudden, you are basically whatever is on the screen," said Michela Alioto. That is important to Alioto because not only is she a successful young woman who worked at the White House as a member of Vice President Al Gore's domestic policy team but she is unable to walk as a result of a ski lift accident that occurred in 1981.

For women business owners who have historically had less access to capital to build their businesses, technology creates a new scenario where small start-ups can compete with the big boys. According to the NFWBO, women entrepreneurs are taking a more proactive approach than men are in their adoption of new technology and the use of the Internet to grow their businesses. Women business owners who have established a home page for their business tripled from 1996 to 1997.[3] Deals are being closed and alliances built, spanning thousands of miles, through cyberspace.

Women entrepreneurs can effectively utilize technology to build business empires right from their own homes. In Waukesha, Wisconsin, Deb Edlhuber ships packages of wildflower seeds all over the country. If you visit her Web site at www.prairiefrontier.com, you would never know that she works from home in her slippers.

"CNBC called and they couldn't believe I'm this little company. My business has really taken off since I've been on the Internet, and when I started I didn't know the first thing about what I was doing. But so many women could do what I'm doing. The Internet presents a great opportunity. Women have to realize if you can present information in a pleasing way, then things will work and you'll be successful," explained Edlhuber.

"I think it's probably the most revolutionary thing that has happened. It's a great advantage for women because with the cost of technology plummeting, there's no excuse not to have the most powerful computers and the latest modems and the most gorgeous printers. I think it's imperative to make sure you have everything you need to compete at a very high level. It's much easier to take the leap when you're not worried about looking small, unprofessional, or foolish," said Jane Applegate.

"All [of] our surveys show that a woman [who] has a business that may only be $500,000 in revenue can compete with a much larger business if she is on the cutting edge of technology," said Edie Fraser.

Angie Kim, president and chief customer officer of Equal Footing.com, says the technology revolution is opening up incredible opportunities for women in all fields, particularly in e-commerce. "E-commerce with its equalizing effects, makes it easier to cut through the glass ceiling that has hindered women in the old economy," she said.

However, Kim cautions that a gender gap could occur easily in this burgeoning new marketplace. "Currently, many of the emerging technology leaders are men, due to the fact that women have, as a general matter, steered away from engineering, computer sciences, and other technology-focused fields. In order to take full advantage of the opportunities available to women, we must encourage girls not to be afraid of technology and the sciences," she continued.

Women not only use technology for entrepreneurial endeavors, but they also use it to structure more flexible work schedules. As corporate America strives to keep talented women in the workforce, technology offers an attractive solution.

"Financial equality worldwide will increase dramatically in the next ten years with the advent of e-commerce and Internet connections. Prior to this time, men had the upper edge, particularly because they could devote more time to work, and they were more willing to exert themselves to exhaustion. However, today, when a large percentage of commerce will be done via computer, women can have flexible hours, and be more efficient with their time and achieve much greater success," said John Gray, author of *Men Are from Mars, Women Are from Venus: A Practical Guide for Improving Communication and Getting What You Want in Your Relationships.*[4]

"Technology gives you flexibility. It opens up options to us so that we can basically do what we want and do it all," said Michela Alioto.

In addition to flexibility and business opportunities, the Internet creates a forum where women can reach out to each other. Women from all corners of the world can join together to help each other. Friendships and mentoring relationships are developed via this new world of technology.

One of my mentors lives hundreds of miles away, yet with the ease of the Internet, she could be my next-door neighbor. We can strategize and share information with the mere click of a mouse. By connecting through cyberspace, you broaden your information base because you meet women from all walks of life and from divergent backgrounds. No matter what profession you have chosen or what business you are in, you are not isolated when you reach out through the Internet. For women who have been excluded from traditional male networks, this is an important development.

Finally, the Internet is an information resource, and it has democratized the process. Access to information no longer depends on your position or status. You can find anything you need to know about any subject, and you never have to leave your desk. What previously took hours of research at a library, can be easily accessed through cyberspace. Effortlessly you can stay abreast of the latest market trends, monitor your competitors, follow financial news, and catch up on current events. That is important because, as we all know, information is power.

Nancy Roath, vice president of software marketing at IBM

Corporation, decided that she wanted to purchase a new Jeep Chero-kee. She went online and researched the trade-in value of her current car, and what the dealer cost was on the new model she wanted to buy. She also discovered that a $1,000 rebate was being offered from the manufacturer to the dealer. Armed with this information, she went to a local Jeep dealership.

"When I pulled up, I saw the exact model, color, everything I wanted. So I walked in and a salesman approached. I pointed to the car, and said, 'I want to buy that car, I want to pay 'X' amount for it, and I have about forty-five minutes.' He escorted me into his office, and of course, he began to deal. He went back and forth a few times to the manager, before I grew impatient and marched right to the manager myself. I explained what I wanted, and substantiated my price with the information I had. Within my forty-five-minute time frame, I had a new car," Roath said.

Information and knowledge are key wealth creators. Finally, thanks to technology, the scales are beginning to tip in a woman's favor.

Education—Your Most Prized Possession

"If a man empties his purse into his head, no man can take it from him."

—Benjamin Franklin

You can lose your car, your husband, your house, your friends, and your job, but no matter what happens, no one can ever take away your education.

Frequently, women find they must be better qualified than a man to get ahead. Impressive educational credentials give you a def-inite edge in the competitive business world. In my opinion, there is nothing more important than a quality education. An education not only helps you to succeed professionally, but it also personally en-hances your life by opening up new worlds and insights.

In today's marketplace, it is difficult to succeed without at least a college degree. A college degree today is equivalent to a high school diploma a few decades ago. The real competitive advantage comes from ongoing training and postgraduate work.

When Sharon Hadary was working in the personnel research department of a large corporation, she learned that an advanced degree would be her ticket to future opportunities. "The director of the department took me aside, and told me my biggest problem as a woman in industry is that women don't have any credibility. So if you really want to have credibility you need to get a doctorate. I thanked him for the great advice and went back to school. Today, his comments would be totally inappropriate, but that was the way it was back then," said Hadary.

Things haven't changed much since Hadary's early days in the business world, even though there isn't any hard evidence to support that fact. However, research shows that two-thirds of the women at the highest corporate levels have postgraduate degrees.[5]

"Today you need a college education and you almost need to have a master's or a doctorate to get the good, high-paying jobs. Women need many more plusses on our side of the aisle than men do. We are still playing catch-up here, and we still have to emphasize the fact that education is the one way that we're going to actually move up," said Michela Alioto.

Obtaining an advanced degree can be a personal sacrifice. When I went to law school, I worked full-time and attended class at night. I understand firsthand how much you give up because for four years, I had no real life. But it was one of the best things that I have ever done.

"To be competitive today, whether you are a man or a woman, you have to have continuing education. It's critical for anybody who is a professional. I believe that learning is a daily process, and it's the only way to get to excellence," said Edie Fraser.

Educational credentials demonstrate you have the commitment and dedication to achieve a goal, which sets you a step above the rest. In the business world, that is important and a good indicator of continued success.

"I really pushed my kids, and I'm glad I did. I have a daughter who is an attorney. I have another daughter whom I forced to get a degree, and when she wanted to back away, I said, 'I don't care what you do, but you're going to get the degree. It shows the world that you know how to complete the circle,'" said Eric Segal.

Educational credentials ensure that you will be taken more seriously in business. I love to watch men's faces when they learn that I am an attorney. You can actually see them make the mental adjustment from assuming I am a secretary to putting me in the category of someone to be reckoned with.

Education is a prized possession that will enhance every aspect of your life.

Read Everything You Can Get Your Hands On

Learning does not stop once you have completed your formal education. You may have a diploma to hang on the wall, but that is not enough. Learning is an ongoing daily process. How many books have you read lately? How many magazines do you read?

You probably rationalize that you have so much to read at work that you don't have the time or the desire to read anything else. But, you can't afford not to read. In this fast-paced and rapidly changing economy, reading is a survival strategy. Reading broadens your horizons. There is a great line in the movie *Working Girl*, starring Melanie Griffith. Griffith's character, a department secretary, is explaining how it was she, not her boss, who came up with the idea for a merger of two broadcasting giants. She says the idea originated from two newspaper articles. After all, she explained, "You never know where the really big ideas will come from."

Shelly Spiegal, founder and president of Search communications, an online clearinghouse for college admissions videos, reads forty publications every month. "People ask how I can possibly do all this reading, but I can't *not* do it," she said in an October 2000 *Entrepreneur* magazine article.

The world is changing so rapidly today that if you don't open your mind to new ideas and information, you will never survive. The broader your information base is, the more knowledgeable, credible, and creative you will be. You should strive to be well versed in a myriad of topics. Pick up a variety of magazines at your local newsstand, and read them cover to cover. Force yourself to read articles about new subjects—even subjects about which you think you have no interest. You will be amazed at what you will learn, and how you may be able to utilize that information in the future.

In addition to becoming a voracious reader, continue to broaden and enhance your skills. Be adventurous—try new things. Consider enrolling in a foreign language course at a local community college, or take a quantum physics seminar. How about a tap dancing class?

At Southwestern Bell, Barbara Wilkinson's willingness to learn new things helped her to advance her career. She was asked to move into data processing, yet as a foreign language major in college, she had never completed a computer course. That did not stop Wilkinson from taking the new position. Instead, she took the job and enrolled in an introductory data processing course.

"Just because you didn't spend four years in college studying something doesn't mean you can't still do it," advised Wilkinson. "I learned the fundamentals of computer programming from the academic courses, and could then better manage a group of skilled programmers. I was familiar with the business requirements, and together we could develop the computer systems to support those functions. There are lots of ways to make up for technical or other knowledge areas that initially you may be lacking. Just go do it."

"You have to be constantly moving and growing and learning, and you never want to stop. Whether you're taking classes or you're reading business books or magazines or taking seminars or whatever, you've got to stay in action because you can get out of the mainstream too quickly," said Beverly Berner.

Never underestimate the power of a good, creative idea. Just make sure it comes from you.

Break through the Mundane—Color outside the Lines

In 1899, the director of the U.S. Patent office Charles Duell announced that the office might as well be closed. "Everything that can be invented has been invented," he explained.

Duell's comment seems silly today since we have just witnessed a century with the most rapid change in history. Yet, you may fall prey to the same paralyzing attitude when you insist on living in the past. To be successful, you can't be reactive to a changing marketplace, you must be proactive. You need the tools to anticipate change and position yourself on the leading edge.

"Speed is one of the fundamental characteristics of the new economy. Everything happens quickly, so we really have to improvise more and more. Things are changing so fundamentally, there really aren't any guidelines. You just have to make it up as you go," explained Juanita Weaver, a creativity consultant who is based in the Washington, D.C., area.

Because the world is rapidly changing around us, it is impossible to know and control everything. A further complication is the reality that the old tried-and-true methods of doing business aren't effective anymore. If you adhere to traditional ways of thinking and business methodologies, you will trudge inside the status quo, which is destined for failure. Forget what you learned in business school and instead let your creative juices flow. Your ability to think creatively—to give yourself permission to color outside the lines—is a critical business skill.

Don't worry if you have never considered yourself the creative type. All of us are born with an abundance of creativity, but we lose it as we grow older. We hear, "No, you can't do it that way," so many times that we give up. To tap into your creativity, forget all the reasons why you can't do something, and open your mind to new possibilities. Stretch your imagination.

Women are generally strong creative thinkers because, according to research, we are right-brained thinkers.[6] The right side of the brain is responsible for creativity. The majority of men are left-brained thinkers, which means they think more linearly. In a business environment where creativity is a strategic asset, women have an opportunity to excel.

Creative thinking is about having the courage to look at issues from a new perspective and to question conventional attitudes. Historically, those who radically tested the boundaries of proven strategies were considered eccentric or lunatics because our educational system teaches us reproductive thinking. Reproductive thinking involves formulas and memorization. We've been taught to believe that a certain action will always get the same reaction. However, we can't rely on that kind of predictability in the new economy.

Creative thinking is productive thinking. Productive thinking gives you the freedom to experiment and challenge existing principles. You are rewarded for ideas, not parroting back information. Productive thinking involves the ability to look at a situation from every possible angle without fear of condemnation. And it requires you to challenge preexisting assumptions based on past knowledge.

"One of the keys to thinking creatively is to be in the moment. You know, get out of the past and [into] the future. If you can be in the moment and fully present, you're not reacting to your old ideas, your adaptations, or previous learned behaviors, you're having a direct experience with something," Juanita Weaver explained.

Creativity trainers encourage you to tap into your internal child to capture your creativity. They ask you to become a curious observer of your environment and to examine each life experience as though it were the first. Be curious and ask questions like a young child—ask how, why, when, where, and how. Don't close yourself off. Avoid the temptation to reject an idea because its seems odd or different.

To be creative, you must be in the right frame of mind, and that means you can't be under stress. "If you tighten up, you'll be blocked on a physical as well as a mental level. You're not as agile or strong. You're not creative," Weaver explained.

Relax. Try taking a walk, listening to your favorite music, or meditating to get in touch with yourself. The goal is to feel playful and childlike, not anxious and tensed up.

Successful Women Thrive on Competition

Dr. Sylvia Rimm, a psychologist and researcher at Case Western University, wrote a book called *See Jane Win*. She interviewed more than one thousand successful women and found that competition was important to them. It is not true, she wrote, that women are not competitive. The successful women featured in her book had grown up participating in competitive situations, such as sports or essay contests. As a result, these women learned a lot about successfully functioning in a competitive world. They knew what it was like to win as well as to lose.

"Many of our successful women listed 'winning in competition' as an important positive experience for them," Rimm said in her book.

Competition is a word that has pejorative connotations for many women. Most likely, it is because many women did not participate in competitive activities as young girls. It has only been recently that competitive sports have been widely accepted and available to women. Many women grew up with an understanding that good girls don't compete with one another.

Competition and business work together to place women who aren't comfortable with competition at a clear disadvantage. That is something Jane Applegate realized when she decided to become a journalist. "In journalism, you are competing against a member of your own team as well as competing against people from other newspapers. The whole business is very competitive, and I think I just learned how to fend for myself from that. I guess I always knew that if I was going to be a reporter. I was going to have to learn [how] to elbow my way to the front of the room at all the press conferences. Competition was just the nature of the business," she explained.

Competition has always been a part of my life. I grew up competing, not in sports but in talent competitions, and I became a much tougher critic of myself than any judge. Second place was never satisfactory. Friends and foes often describe me as the quintessential overachiever. My personal philosophy is based on the old adage, "If you are resting on your laurels, you have them in the wrong place." Success is a daily journey, and you should always challenge yourself to do better.

Competition isn't a negative—it is an energy force that pushes you to continually strive for excellence, both personally and professionally. The negative aspects of competition result from the unethical behavior of people who want to win at the expense of others. That is not the essence of the competitive spirit.

"There are people I work with, and people I went to college with at the University of Pennsylvania, that are aggressively competitive. They would do anything they could to get a leg up on you, to get that job, even if it meant climbing on you. I never felt like I had to step on people to move ahead. I just worked on making myself better," said Heather Dorf, a CNN/Fn field producer.

Are you born with a competitive spirit? I think some of us are. But that does not mean you can't learn to thrive in a competitive environment. No one can teach you to be competitive, but you can't win unless you are. There is nothing like winning. Winning is exhilarating.

Competition energizes Catherine Garda Newton, who has worked in competitive environments her entire career, first as an executive with IBM, then as an American Express financial adviser, and now as CEO of her own firm. "Being in a competitive situation means you are pitting your wits against something or someone, and I love it. But, I think some women avoid it because it's an uncomfortable feeling. You can sit back and recognize those feelings of discomfort and then learn to manage them," she said.

"I always liked to play in sports, and I was always competitive academically. That competitive nature has served me well. It allowed me to step out, take the risk, and move out of my comfort zone in different situations," explained Barbara Wilkinson.

If you are uncomfortable in a competitive environment, get

over it. You will never achieve the professional success and power you desire without the ability to compete. Tap into your competitive spirit and let it guide you to the top.

Become a Networking Queen

"Women have always been good networkers; they just used to call it their Christmas list."

—Juanita Weaver

The good ole boys' network controls business and politics as it has done for centuries. There is no special criterion for membership in the boys club other than your gender. Becoming a member is a rite of passage for young boys as they emerge from adolescence and step into manhood. However, membership in the boys club has definite advantages. As a member of the club, you are privy to important information, and many critical business decisions are based on the club's membership roster. Regular meetings of the club are held on the golf course, in the men's room, or in a smoke-filled cigar bar. A fraternity-like atmosphere exists among the club's members, and there is a sign on the door that reads, "No women allowed." Exclusion from the informal good old boys' network continues to bar women from top management.[7]

Historically, women have had no comparable alternative to the good ole boys' club. There weren't any female organizations relating to business, and most of the professional and civic organizations, such as the Rotary, did not allow women members. The brave women in the workplace found themselves isolated and alone, particularly those who had aspirations for advancement.

"After World War II, my dad came home from the war and said these women don't have any network. He realized the network was men's way of connecting outside of the workplace and he wanted to create that for women, so he founded the American Business Women's Association," said Carolyn Elman.

Today there are thousands of women's organizations ranging from the broad-based, such as the ABWA or the National Association of Female Executives, to the more specific, such as the Women Lawyer's Association or Women in Agriculture. These organizations provide support and an opportunity to learn and share information. Additionally, women's organizations offer an opportunity to get considerable practice in developing leadership skills. By accepting leadership positions within these groups, women can demonstrate their ability to excel and gain visibility for themselves.

Belonging to one of the many women's organizations is an important first step in building your network. But a real networking queen knows there is more involved in building a network than joining a club.

"Women don't know how to be good old boys. Men know how to move around and make sure they get the business to their buddy," said Marsha Serlin.

You probably already have the foundation of a personal network. Think about the number of acquaintances you have from work, industry associations, church, and charitable organizations. However, if you are like most women, you probably don't use 90 percent of these contacts. These associates and friends can be the beginning of your personal network.

However, a truly strong personal network is not built from a list of mere acquaintances. Juanita Weaver is a true networking queen. She has an address book that looks like the New York City white pages. While she seems to know everyone, what is most impressive is that most people refer to her as a good friend. What is her secret? She says it is creating a human connection.

"That doesn't mean I don't talk to a lot of people, but I really try to come home with one special connection," she explained. "I am always interested in the other person as a person and not just as a contact, and I think people feel that difference."

Effective networking is time-consuming, and you may think that you are too busy managing your home, your family, and your business to find time. If your goal is have success and power, then you can't afford not to network. You never know when you will meet someone who will be instrumental in helping you to achieve your goals.

The number of networking events, professional association meetings, civic groups, and charitable events in any given week can be overwhelming. Don't drive yourself crazy trying to hit them all—be smart. Carefully select the events that you believe are the best fit for you both personally and professionally.

"I would figure out what kind of contacts are most useful to your particular business, and think broadly. You don't just want to know people in your industry. You want to know people in a lot of different areas. In today's marketplace, connections with all kinds of groups and organizations and industries are becoming more and more important," Juanita Weaver suggested.

One of the most important things to remember about building a network is to give before you get. If you go to an event and focus on handing out cards to a million people in anticipation of getting immediate results, you will be disappointed. Focus instead on how you may be of assistance to someone else, and in turn, the rewards will come your way.

Additionally, as you are building your network, stay in contact with the people you meet. Communication is the glue that holds your network together. Take time to write personal notes. Sincere personal notes have a tremendous and long-lasting impact. I've been told that is one of the mechanisms George W. Bush used to build his vast personal network.

The advantages of a far-reaching network are numerous—one of which is knowing the right person to call when you need help. Whether you are looking for a doctor, hairdresser, new supplier, new employee, banker, or a great restaurant, you at least have a place to start and a minimal connection with someone who can point you in the right direction.

"I've heard it called the power of weak connections. If you look at somebody who has gotten a job—how many of them know the person who hired them? Not many. It's usually because somebody recommended them. It is not that the person recommending was necessarily best friends with the person doing the hiring, maybe they only see each other twice a year, but there is a connection," Weaver explained.

In an ideal world, opportunities would come our way because of our talent and abilities. But we do not live in an ideal world, and it is not what you know but whom your know. Build a strong net-work—and become a networking queen.

Be Inclusive, Not Exclusive

Many women question the benefits of belonging to women-only groups, while other women swear by them. However, when women splinter off from the mainstream into their own enclaves, are they further perpetuating the division between men and women in the workplace?

The answer is that women really need a little of both. Women's organizations provide a haven where women can support each other and comfortably discuss issues that impact their lives. As a facilita-tor for the Women Presidents' Organization, an exclusive group of women business owners whose members serve as business advisers to one another, I have watched many of the organization's members switch from coed advisory groups to the exclusive women-only scenario. One woman said she prefers the women-only environment because she knows the other women will understand when she needs to cry.

"Women behave differently when they are with all women than when they are with a mixed group, so I think they recognize that and seek out women's groups," said Carolyn Elman.

Women's groups have their role and purpose, but structuring an exclusive good ole girls' network to compete with the good ole boys' club is not a smart idea. The most effective network you can build is diverse. To facilitate change and create greater opportunities for yourself and other women, you must mainstream. Your strategy should include supporting other women, but, at the same time, you want to knock down the doors of the men's club so you can begin competing on an equal basis. Inclusiveness, not exclusiveness, is the strength of a strong personal network.

"The interesting thing about the professional women's group at Southwestern Bell is our membership is not limited to women. If you are going to recognize and take advantage of the benefits that a diverse employee population offers, then it doesn't make sense for us to create exclusive organizations," said Barbara Wilkinson.

What is your reaction when you walk into a room where you are one of only a few women? Do you automatically assume the men are the ones with the power? Do you migrate toward other women because that is less intimidating?

"I am not a member of the old boys network, but I don't let that stop me. When I'm at a commercial finance meeting or somewhere like that, I don't sit around with a small group of women. I make sure I go up and introduce myself to the men and make them talk to me. I've gotten to know some interesting people who have helped me along the way," said Kay Berry.

"I'll never be in the men's locker rooms. Let's face it, I'm not going to get there. I'm okay with that, even though it would probably be good for me to be there. But I am, as much as I can be, one of the boys," explained Marsha Serlin.

Notes

1. "Straight Talk," *Working Woman*, www.workingwoman.com/article/article.html?id109&cid81&tidarticle—generic, September 18, 1999.
2. Mark Borden, "Thinking about Tomorrow," *Fortune*, November 22, 1999, p. 170.
3. Taken from a press release, "Embracing the Information Age: A Comparison of Women and Men Business Owners," National Foundation for Women Business Owners, September 30, 1997.
4. "Expert Forecast: Will Women Ever Gain Employment Parity with Men?" *The Wall Street Journal*, January 1, 2000, p. R36.
5. Taken from a research report, "Women in Corporate Leadership: Progress and Prospects," Catalyst Research, 1996.

6. Taken from a press release, "Styles of Success, The Thinking and Management Styles of Women and Men Business Owners," National Foundation for Women Business Owners, July 19, 1994.
7. Taken from a research report, "Women in Corporate Leadership: Progress and Prospects," Catalyst Research, 1996.

THE POWER OF BALANCE

"That the birds of worry and care fly above your head, this
you cannot change; but that they build nests in your hair, this
you can prevent."

—Chinese Proverb

Be a Superstar, Not a Superwoman

"I worked on that report until 2:00 A.M. this morning. And I worked all day Saturday and Sunday."

"I can't go to the gym tonight. I have to stay and finish this report."

"I have a million things to do. There aren't enough hours in the day."

"A vacation? Who has time to take a vacation?"

Does this sound like you? If your answer is yes, then you are trying to be a superwoman. You are operating under the misperception that people are impressed by your ability to juggle so many projects at once, and that they admire your energy and strong work ethic. Assuming anyone even notices what you are doing, they probably think you are crazy, and they are tired of hearing about how hard you work all the time. It's not cool to be a superwoman anymore.

Unless you thrive on panic attacks and enjoy the agony of ulcers and migraine headaches, then it is time to take control of your life. Wise up and realize that you can't do it all—at least, not all at the same time. Give the superwoman routine a rest, and focus instead on becoming a superstar, which means you are going to have to make some changes. Superstars are women who expertly manage their lives to their advantage so that they can achieve their personal best. They are the ones with the power.

"I Can Handle It!"

If you are suffering from the superwoman complex, then you are most likely drowning in a sea of endless projects, paperwork, correspondence, and routine tasks, but you would never think of asking for help because you've got that "I can handle it" attitude. Successful women know how to do what is essential, and they delegate the rest.

"I'm only successful because of the people around me. I choose good people who can fill in the voids [of the skills] that I don't have because you can't be everything to everybody. That's the trick," explained Barbara Dressel, CEO of Automark.

Delegation is what I call the *mytop* theory—multiply yourself through other people. When you delegate, you enhance your own productivity and effectiveness by utilizing the skills and talents of others. Plus, you will enjoy the added benefit of not being so stressed out all the time.

Delegation is difficult for most women, especially women entrepreneurs. We have a propensity to be perfectionists; therefore, we are reluctant to let go. But if you don't reach out for help, you get bogged down in laborious details or time-intensive tasks, while others leap ahead like gazelles.

"When someone asks me if there is anything I wish I could do over, I would say I wish I'd been more willing to let go sooner. You get to a point when you can't do everything, but you think you can. I just thought my business couldn't afford expensive consultants. But that really wasn't true. I just hadn't come to terms with sharing control. I waited too long, and as I look back, I think we could have grown faster, smarter, and much bigger. As it was, we had three successful divisions within the company, but we still should have moved faster, and when I decided to pay the price and seek the best help, it made a huge difference," explained Flori Roberts, founder of Flori Roberts Cosmetics.

"You just have to take the plunge. You will always think that things will work out better if you do them yourself, but as you get busier, the reality is it's not going to get done. You have to delegate freely. Because if you don't learn that, you will not be able to balance your family or personal pursuits or anything outside of work. Delegating is absolutely the key," said Bonnie Glatzer, a partner in the law firm Thelen, Reid, and Priest.

Perfectionism is paralyzing and can jeopardize your success. When you try to maintain control over everything yourself, eventually something will fall through the cracks. One of the first things I learned when I began supervising people was that just because something wasn't done exactly as I would have done it, that doesn't mean that it is wrong—it's just different. Not everything has to be done exactly "my way." However, that does not mean you should relinquish control over the end result.

Remember that no one person can be good at everything. If you can recognize your strengths, then surround yourself with people who complement your talents, you will be more successful.

Let me tell you the story about the New Forest School. Enrolled in this school, which is hidden among the trees, are the squirrel, the rabbit, and the fish. There are three courses at the school: swimming, hopping, and tree climbing. Now, the rabbit excels in hopping but just can't get the hang of tree climbing, so they put her in remedial tree climbing and made her spend all her time trying to learn to climb a tree. Then, there is the squirrel who happens to be a very good tree climber but can't swim a lick. But, of course, they make her spend all her time trying to swim. Finally, the fish makes straight As in swimming but fails miserably in the hopping class, so once again all her time and energy are spent on hopping. The result is that all three students get frustrated and drop out.

You don't want to be so frustrated that you eventually give up. Surround yourself with good people who have diverse talents, skill levels, and backgrounds. A skilled delegator identifies the people with the necessary skills and experience and then empowers these people by giving them the responsibility and accountability to get the job done.

"I think one of the characteristics of leaders is they develop other leaders who can respond to a clearly defined mission and goals, and then take charge and run with it," explained Barbara Wilkinson, vice president of external affairs with Southwestern Bell.

A word of warning. Once you have delegated a project or a task, be careful not to become a micromanager. "It's something I struggle with today. It's probably taken me a good twenty years to learn to pull back and say everybody's competent at something. Let everybody else have a chance to shine. If people come to you after that opportunity has been given or created, and then they say, 'We'd like your input,' that's quite different. I try very hard not to be, as my father used to say, a steamroller," said Linda Jacobsen, president of Global Vision Strategies.

Knowing what types of projects to delegate is critical. Take a look at your workload, and begin by unloading tasks that can easily be done by someone else, particularly administrative tasks. Some women won't delegate the "grunt" work because they feel uncomfortable asking someone else to do it. So they continue to grind it out, wasting valuable time and impacting their performance. Think about it from an economic viewpoint. Consider your earning capacity and how much it costs your company or your employer for you to sit at your desk cranking out routine sales letters. In a cost/benefit analysis, you are better off doing something that requires more skill and directly impacts the bottom line.

Once you have passed along the miscellaneous tasks, focus on which projects utilize your strengths and are essential functions to achieve the overall result. Delegate those things that are not essential elements and do not utilize your strengths.

While running an Edward Jones investment office in South Carolina, Stephanie Simmons realized that to successfully build her business she needed to focus on her two greatest strengths: working with people and teaching. At the same time, she acknowledged that creativity and organization are not her fortes, and in those areas, she could use some help.

"So what I did was I put together a support team. I hired an assistant who is very organized. She understands technology and her files are unbelievable. She takes copious notes on every phone call, and she keeps me in line. Then, I hired a marketing assistant to help with creative marketing strategies. This frees my time up to do my teaching and dealing with my clients one-on-one," she explained.

Successful and powerful women know how to work smarter, not harder. Delegate, delegate, delegate! You will be amazed at how much more time you have to take care of yourself and how much more successful you will be.

Hire a Cleaning Lady

I don't really mean to literally go out and hire a cleaning lady. However, if you don't have one, trust me, it is the way to go. What I am talking about is developing a cadre of resources that can help you manage your personal life and keep you from losing your mind. You need a list of caterers, party planners, tailors, dog walkers, dry cleaning services that pick up and deliver, courier services, and personal shoppers. Keep these names and telephone numbers handy. Then, when you wind up in a bind because you were invited to a friend's birthday party and you haven't had time to shop for a gift, or you don't have "a thing to wear," you are prepared with reinforcements. It is all about knowing where and how to best utilize your time and energy so that you can have balance in your life.

During a meeting that I attended with a group of highly successful women in the financial services, I was stunned to learn how many of them felt guilty about hiring housekeeping services. As Bobbe Suhocki, a partner in Edward Jones, a brokerage company, explained, when she started her career, she really believed she could manage everything. "I had always kept a very clean house, cooked meals for my family, everything. Then, my business took off, and I just couldn't do it all. Finally, I broke down and hired some help. It was the best thing I've ever done, but I really felt guilty at first," she said.

Managing your personal life is as important to your success as managing your business. Get over the guilt and hire a cleaning lady. Use those extra hours to make one more sales call, take your kids to a movie, enjoy a romantic dinner with your husband, or better yet, go get a massage.

Go with Your Gut

"Every day you have decisions to make—should you go left or right. Someone says left, but you have this feeling that you should really go right. But you end up keeping your mouth shut because you think maybe you don't have all the facts. However, your gut is telling you to go right. Then, it turns out you should have gone right. When that happens, 100 percent of the time—my gut was right. I tend to assume that I didn't understand something correctly or didn't read it right, and I back down. I think when women feel free to trust their instincts and begin to lead and not back down, we'll be in high demand," said Sarah Hudanich, a former computer company executive.

Women are intuitive thinkers, yet many of us, like Hudanich, do not trust our own instincts. How many times have you known something was a mistake going into it, but you did it anyway? While in a new management position at Bank One, Vanessa Freytag inherited an employee who, she was told, was having problems. She met with the person and her initial reaction was that this particular employee was not going to be able to turn things around. However, like so many women, she ignored her instincts.

"I was wrong. My first impression was right. The person was just unhappy and blamed everyone else but himself, and it didn't change. So we went down the road of having to get into issues of disciplinary action because the performance didn't improve and finally the individual left. So, not trusting my instincts actually came back to bite me. My instincts are almost always right, and I kick myself afterward if I've ignored them," she said.

Women fail to trust their instincts because we lack confidence in our own abilities. Additionally, we worry too much about pleasing and taking care of other people. We are nurturers and rescuers. Our decisions are often based on what we think we should do, rather than on what feels right.

A sociology professor once said to me, "Think with your head, feel with your heart, but go with your gut." As a college student, I didn't appreciate the wisdom of his advice, but his words have nonetheless stuck with me throughout the years. Now, I think we would all be well advised to follow his wisdom.

Follow Your Passion

Learning to trust your instincts not only helps you make better business decisions, but it also enhances your personal decision making. Women can lose themselves in the roles others expect them to play—wife, mother, daughter, professional, volunteer, etc. It is easy to ignore or postpone your own needs and desires until they almost cease to exist. Then, you wonder why you aren't happy. If you listen to your inner voice, it can guide you along the path to success. When you follow your own true passion, you will be happier and everyone else around you will prosper as a result.

"Women are still finding their way in terms of how do you

design a life that you really want. How do we nurture ourselves, our friends, our husbands and our careers? What I'm working with women on is how you can be everything to yourself and then how does that show up with everybody else," said Laura Finestone, founder and president of VIA Associates.

Barbara Dressel insists there are some things in your life that simply are not negotiable. She says that once you have an understanding of what those things are, write them down. "Then, you'll have a snapshot of exactly what you want and suddenly it evolves. I applied for a job once, and after I applied for the job, instinctively I knew I was going to be a square peg in a round hole there. It wasn't going to work, so I walked away from it. It's okay to walk away from stuff. It doesn't make you a bad person," she explained.

A woman needs to maintain her true essence according to Karen Harriman, vice president of marketing and development for a regional health care company. "Moses didn't bring [down] from the mount the '10 Commandments' of being a good mother and wife. Women must instinctively learn to adapt to these roles. Women have to be careful of not losing themselves in these roles. The most important rule for taking on multiple roles is to not lose that core person."

Kay Berry is a good example of someone who stuck to her core values and followed her passion. Berry once worked for a company where the owner thought women should be at home, not in the office. Every year the owner went to Europe for six weeks. During one of his junkets overseas, Berry made a sale to a big company that her company hadn't done business with for three years. Masterfully, she put all the details together for the job only to have the owner take over the account when he returned.

"You know I didn't really care about getting a commission; I just wanted the recognition for getting the job. But I didn't get a thing. At that point I knew I couldn't stay there a day longer. I told him to take his job and do you know what with it. Then, I went home to tell my husband of six months and my three kids that I had just quit my job, and I wasn't going back to work until I found something I really wanted to do. I realized I had to be true to myself and do what was right for me. I pretty much go on my gut instincts. I think that is probably why I have been so successful today," she explained.

An insurance salesman his entire life, Iris Salsman's father made a good living, but he hated what he did for a living. "It affected him that he hated it so much, and he had a certain degree of bitterness and regret. That's what made me realize that the worst thing in life is doing something you don't like, or that's unfulfilling. Of course you have to make a living, but you have to have some personal satisfaction, too," Salsman said.

As CEO of Ogilvy and Mather, one of the world's largest advertising firms, Shelly Lazarus is a role model for young women. She says the most fundamental advice she can share with everyone is to try to find something you love to do, because you cannot lead in business or hope to find balance in life without that.[1]

"Don't get sucked into living your life based on what others want you to do. Think about what it is you want for yourself. Ask yourself, 'Is this really going to juice me up or get me excited?' That's the key," claimed Catherine Garda Newton, CEO of Bearoness Creations, Inc.

Passion is the driving force behind greatness. It is what gives you the energy to get up early and go to bed late. There is no true success without passion. Grant yourself permission to follow your passion—to be successful and to do what makes you happy. If you are happy and enjoy what you are doing, others around you will be happy too. Personal power comes from taking care of yourself first.

Defining Success Creates Personal Power

"There is only one success—to be able to spend your life in your own way."

—Christopher Morley, American writer

Success in the business world has long been defined by white males because they dominated the game. They made the rules, and they kept score. Think about it, What is the first thing that comes to mind when you think of success? Wealth, power, status, fame?

Before you read on, write down the name of someone whom you consider to be very successful, either dead or alive. Does the successful person you named have wealth and/or power? Now, write down what success means to you. Are those things included in your personal definition of success?

There is an interesting dichotomy with women when it comes to this exercise. Most frequently, when women do this exercise in my seminars I find their definitions of success don't focus on money, status, or power, but the successful individual they select usually has one or more of those characteristics.

Success is a relative term, and for women, success is multidimensional. Certainly, professional achievement is part of our definition, but typically women include other aspects such as family, friends, and quality of life. More and more women are creating life goals measured in their own terms, rather than succumbing to the expectations of others. Successful women know how to get in touch with who they are and what they want.

"Success is not just an achievement one earns in the business field. It's more important to achieve success in your family life. It can be measured by such simple things as knowing you have raised a good citizen, or hearing the words 'I love you, Mom or honey' every day without prompting or having your son or daughter tell you how proud he or she is of Mom. The reward of that success is pride; the investment to earn that reward is time and sacrifice," explained Karen Harriman.

When Sarah Hudanich first joined IBM, she said she met wonderful, professional people who seemed to move up to the middle management level and then stop there. She could not understand why these people didn't push to the top, and she viewed this as a failure. But, over the years, she has changed her view to focus more on life success than career success. "I think women tend to take a look at their whole life, whereas men compartmentalize it. Even my male peers today seem to look at their career, and as they move up the corporate ladder, they always take jobs that increase their recognition or one-up their last job. But a lot of my peer women don't. That's probably because as women carry the burden of both career and family, young children as well as [the] elderly, and you can't do it all. My mother-in-law used to tell me, 'You can do it all, just not all at the same time,' and I bucked that for a long time. Now I see she's right," explained Hudanich.

"I evaluate a person not by the dollar sign, but what they've done. We keep focusing on the fact that men make the money. But I've come to find out maybe that's true, but at the same time if you prove yourself eventually you'll get what you want, but if you always let the dollar sign hang in front of you, you're never going to be successful. You'll never feel that success," said Barbara Dressel.

"I think women are more willing to step back and say, I'd rather not earn that extra dollar, while there may be more societal pressure on men," Catherine Garda Newton explained.

Women are fortunate because we have so many choices today. We can be career women, own our own businesses, hold public office, serve as the president of a college, or be a stay-at-home mother. Personal fulfillment, success, and power come from sources other than our title and the size of our portfolio.

As women gain more power over their destinies, the traditional arbitrary male definition of success will hopefully evolve to reflect a more feminine, balanced perspective. However, you must have a way of defining your personal success because without knowing what success means to you, how will you know when you have achieved it. Create a definition of success for yourself that captures your personal values and beliefs.

The Power of Pampering

We are all working harder and faster than ever before—some experts say as much as a month per year more. Many of us are finding that we are just plain tired and stressed out. Stress is the number one problem for working women, according to the U.S. Department of Labor. Stress plays havoc on your mental, physical, and emotional well-being. About 75 percent of all doctor visits are for stress-related illnesses, such as headaches, stomach problems, insomnia, or fatigue.

Slow down a little. Stop and smell the roses. Pamper yourself. It is good for your health as well as your productivity and professional success. The concept of pampering as a career-enhancing business tool is catching on, even in large corporations. As companies begin to recognize the need for a little "me" time for their employees, we see the creation of nap rooms, fitness studios, and on-site hair salons.

It does not matter how you "de-stress," as long as you stop and take a break now and then. Do something special that you really enjoy. Try to capture at least an hour every day, and devote that time to yourself. Music is one of my great loves—playing the piano to be specific. After having studied at a music conservatory in college, I let my skills slide over the years. There never seems to be enough time to sit down and play. Then a friend of mine who plays the flute professionally asked me to accompany her in a concert. She dropped off the sheet music, and for the first time in years, I sat down at the piano. At first, my fingers felt still and awkward on the keys, and I was tempted to give up. However, I decided to see if I could rise to the challenge. Slowly, the agility in my fingers began to return and I found I was truly enjoying the diversion from work. Although it was mentally challenging, it was also a stress reliever. For thirty minutes a day, I lost myself in the music and didn't think about work. But the pièce de résistance was the concert itself—performing on stage again. I was in a completely different arena from the business world, and it was invigorating.

If music isn't your thing, find what works best for you: a nice hot bubble bath with lots of candles and a cold glass of champagne, an ambitious game of tennis, or a bicycle ride through the park.

"I have a list of ten things I do everyday that ranges from telling my kids I love them to trying to help someone. I try to read ten pages of a book that I want to read for myself. I take ten minutes at some point in the day, just to do nothing. I listen to one song in a style that's different than I normally do. I really enjoy doing these things," said Vanessa Freytag.

Exercise is a great way to reduce your stress level, but you have to be dedicated. You can't be like the majority of people who make an annual New Year's resolution to get in shape, run out and join a health club, and then quit going after three months. Stay with it. Exercise not only reduces your stress but increases your resistance to disease and helps you fight off those nasty germs you pick up in closed-room meetings or on airplanes. Plus, regular exercise can help you lose weight and look terrific. And when you look good and feel strong and healthy, your confidence level skyrockets.

Whatever you do to relax, make sure it's totally your time, and make sure everyone understands the rules.

As a partner in a law firm, Bonnie Glatzer finds taking time for herself is very important. "I find that if I'm not regularly swimming and doing other things like that, the stress will just kill me. I try to make time for myself. I'm not one of those people who gets mad because I have to sacrifice my whole schedule for the rest of the world. I take yoga twice a week. I go swimming whenever I can. Occasionally I'll have lunch or dinner with a friend. Once in a blue moon I'll even take off a day and go with a girlfriend to a day spa," said Glatzer.

"When I was in my thirties and juggling three schedules—mine, my husband's, and my son's—my sanctuary became my bedroom and bathroom. When I got to a point where I was dead tired and at the end of my rope, I would go in 'my cave' with my favorite book and my family would know that it was my time to be alone. I had to find time outside everyone's daily schedules in order to keep centered and balanced. It just took organization and commitment," said Karen Harriman.

Women entrepreneurs seem to have an even more difficult time finding time for themselves. Their business and their personal lives become so intertwined that it is all-consuming. One woman told me she had been in business for a number of years and thought everything in her life was going well until her husband walked in one day and said he wanted a divorce. When she asked why, he said it was because she never had any time for him. She was so consumed with growing the business that she had failed to nurture their marriage. The good news is that her husband's message was a wake-up call for her, and they were able to work it out. But her story is a good example of how easily our lives can get out of kilter.

Time and time again women entrepreneurs ask me the standard question, "How can I run my business and have a life?" There is no easy answer to that question. If I knew the answer, I would probably be a millionaire. The key is finding what works for you.

As author, columnist, and CEO of SBTV.com, Jane Applegate says she tries to follow the advice she gives in her columns. "I get as much help as I can. I'm very big on getting manicures and pedicures and massages and treating myself well. I'm also totally committed to getting eight or nine hours of sleep a night. There's been a lot of research on that, and I really believe that you can damage your health and hurt your business if you're totally worn out and exhausted all the time. So people make fun of me for having farmer's hours, but I try to be in bed at 9:30 or 10:00 at the latest every night," she explained.

"I belong to a TEC group (The Executive Committee) where we have monthly speakers. One of our speakers was a really terrific guy who sold his business, and now he wants to help other CEOs find balance in their lives. He suggested that every CEO leave for two days on a retreat by themselves and evaluate where they want to be and where they are. No family, no wife, no husband, no nothing and spend some real time looking at yourself," said Marsha Serlin, CEO of United Scrap Metal.

Tapping into your own spirituality can be a good way of relieving stress. Whether or not you are a religious person, devoting time to tune into your inner voice can result in a sense of peace and calmness. "I have quiet time before I come downstairs for breakfast each morning. I've got a couple of daily devotionals and I read those, and I meditate every day. It keeps me centered," said Beverly Berner, a professional business coach.

Finally, take a deep breath and remember you don't have to solve the world's problems today. Instead of feeling guilty about taking special time for yourself, focus on the things that you will reminisce about when you are eighty years old. Will it still be important to you to know you completed that project ahead of schedule, or will you think more fondly of the afternoon you left the office early to take a walk in the park on a beautiful autumn day with a good friend?

"One of the things I realized was that my career was thirty-plus years long. And when you stop and realize that when you are trying to make a decision today, it puts it in perspective. I just stop and think about what will I want to look back [on] over my life and [to] have done? That really helps," said Sarah Hudanich.

Learn to Say No, and Mean It

How many times has someone asked you to do something, either personally or professionally, and you said yes when you really wanted to say no? Women have difficulty saying no. Why? Because we want people to like us. We don't want to hurt anyone's feelings. It is part of the "disease to please."

The more successful you become, the worse it gets. People demand more and more of your time. Will you serve as chairperson for a local charity event? Will you sit on the board of an industry organization? Would you speak to a local women's group? How about chairing your company's United Way campaign? Will you take responsibility for writing up the task force report? Before you know it, you are overwhelmed. Learning to say no, and sticking to your guns, is a necessary survival strategy.

"I get asked to do a million things, and early on I thought I had to do everything in my business. But, I learned to prioritize and put my passions and favorite things where they would most benefit the company and me. After all, you deserve to get some personal pleasure out of your professional life," explained Flori Roberts, founder of Flori Roberts Cosmetics.

"People used to call me and catch me at a moment when I was vulnerable, and I'd say yes. Then, I'd think, Why did I do that? So I've got a great tip, which I've learned over the years. Never, never give an immediate answer when somebody asks you. Tell them you are on another call, or that you need to get back to them in a few days. Then, think about the request and what it entails. Do you have the time to devote to it, and do you want to do it? When I handle it that way, I'm always happy with my decision," said Marsha Serlin.

Serlin offers sound advice. Don't respond immediately; take time to carefully consider the request. If the thought of one more project on your plate throws you into a panic mode, then don't accept it. You can say no in a gracious, but direct fashion. Acknowledge the request in a polite way; then explain you are committed, and you must decline. It is not necessary to provide an elaborate excuse or a detailed explanation, and whatever you do, do not conjure up some fictional story. You will always get caught. A simple no will do. A former business associate of mine proudly displays a sign in his office that says: "What part of no don't you understand?" If someone persists or tries to guilt you into saying yes, remain firm. You have every right to say no. It's your life.

Become a Good Time Manager

The lynchpin of finding balance in your life is developing good time-management skills. Have you ever noticed how the most successful people seem to get the most done, and they still have time to enjoy life? That is because they are good time managers.

"I was on a 24/7 schedule, and then I was diagnosed with rheumatoid arthritis. Boy, does that put things in perspective. I realized I could run my business by working fewer hours and managing my time better. So now I go in at 10:00 A.M. and leave at 4:00 P.M. so

I can spend more time with my daughter. And my business continues to prosper. We're enjoying 10 to 20 percent annual growth," explained Kathy Wood, CEO of Apartment Search.

A long-time friend of mine is always complaining about being stressed out. She claims she never has enough time to get all her work done. Then, in the next breath, she will tell me about going for a long lunch with a friend, getting a manicure and pedicure, or going out for dinner and a night on the town. The simple fact is that she is stressed out because she isn't setting priorities and managing her time.

Get in the habit of creating a "to do" list. When I was working full-time and attending night law school, I became the master of time management. My job was demanding, and I was enrolled in eleven hours per semester at law school. To ensure that I made good grades, I studied about twenty hours every weekend. The only way I was able to ever squeeze anything else in was to live and die by a "to do" list. Every day, I would review my list and set priorities as to what needed to be accomplished that day. The top items I wrote down on a separate index card. Then, I would play a game with myself. The challenge was to get through all the day's priorities, and then try to knock off a few additional items. If I managed to win the game, I would have a special reward for myself. It might be renting my favorite movie, going out to dinner with my husband, or making a trip to a manicurist, but there was always an incentive to give it a little extra push.

Investment representative Stephanie Simmons divides her days into three types: free days, buffer days, and focus days. Focus days, she explained, are the most important. That is where you come up with the three most important activities that make you successful, and you focus only on those activities that day. Simmons found that if you focus 80 percent of your time on these activities, you will be amazed by what you can accomplish. A buffer day is a day where you do what you normally do, and a free day is one spent away from work, doing nothing pertaining to work at all. "What I've found is if I schedule at least one focus day a month, I can triple my business on that day. It goes back to working smarter. It's been a wonderful asset to my business," she explained.

Jane Applegate manages her time by scheduling in- and out-days. "When I lived in Los Angeles, it was difficult just to physically get around town, so I began having what I call in-days and out-days. And I continue to use the same system now. I either stay in the office, literally all day, and I don't leave. So there are days that I'm hunkered down working, doing a little writing, e-mail, and I do most of the business development for my company. Then when I'm out, I'm in Manhattan or Chicago or wherever I'm out. I schedule back-to-back appointments, and I stay out the whole day. So I don't ever really go in and out on the same day. I think that is a really good time-management trick," she said.

There are myriad time-management techniques, and it may take some experimentation to find the one that works best for you. But the key is to always remember to set priorities, take one thing at a time, and stay focused.

Note

1. Anne Thompson, "On Top of the World," *NBC Nightly News,* November 16, 1999.

THE POWER OF ADVOCACY

"Politics is not a spectator sport."

—Congresswoman Barbara Jordan

Recapture the Spirit of a Day Gone By

On August 26, 1920, Congress passed the Nineteenth Amendment to the U.S. Constitution, which gave women, who were 51 percent of the U.S. population, the right to vote. Its passage marked the culmination of a long and difficult battle led by a strong grassroots coalition that became known as the women's suffrage movement. The leaders of this movement were some of the most courageous people this country has ever seen, regardless of race or gender. If you study the women's movement in this country, which I think should be a requirement for all young people, you will find heroic stories of thousands of brave men and women who sacrificed, struggled, and vehemently fought for the rights of all women to be treated equally under the laws of this democracy. Some of these civil rights warriors even landed in jail because they refused to back down from their beliefs.

Simply stated, the women's suffrage movement was founded on the very principles upon which this country was built—that the rights of citizenship should belong to all Americans. However, women do not have equal rights in this country. Sadly today, the passion that fueled the raging fire of that historic fight for equality so many years ago has dwindled to nothing more than glowing embers. Alarmingly, many young women don't understand the magnitude of the fight and have become more or less complacent. So we find that, eight decades after the passage of the Nineteenth Amendment, we continue to struggle with many of the same issues our grandmothers and great-grandmothers fought so hard to eradicate.

In an interview with womenCONNECT.com, UCLA history professor Ellen Carol Dubois said that if Susan B. Anthony and Elizabeth Cady Stanton, early leaders of the women's movement, were here today, they would be delighted at the quality of women's education and at the depth of women's economic achievements. "But they would also help us see how much of what they fought about is still going on: the ways in which women's subordination continues," she stated.

The Underrepresented Majority

The United States ranks thirty-ninth in the world in terms of women in national office.[1] And the number of women in elected positions has leveled off in the past few years. Futurists predict that, at the present rate of progress, it will take as much as half a millennium or more before our "democratic" government, which is supposed to represent all its people, truly achieves representational parity. As a woman, that fact should be alarming to you. Women represent the majority of the population, but we give up our power to men to govern. Haven't men been making the decisions that affect our lives for too long? Yet, women are not getting involved in the political process.

There are myriad reasons why women shun politics. One reason is the stigma attached to politics. Because of Watergate, Iran Contra, Whitewater, Travelgate, and, of course, the infamous Clinton and "what's her name" scandal (I refuse to give her free publicity in this book), which led to the president's impeachment, there is a perceived lack of morality and integrity in government and a growing public disdain for the political process. But apathy and indifference are not the solution.

"Women view politics as dirty. But unless they are involved in it, they are not going to change it. If they believe politics is dirty, then get in there and change it," said Terry Neese, cofounder of Grass-Roots Impact and a national public policy advisor for the National Association of Women Business Owners (NAWBO).

Another reason some women shun the political process is the fear of being labeled a feminist. The "f" word alienates many women because of its association with the radical, bra-burning movement of the early 1970s. If you call a woman a feminist today, you may have a fight on your hands. In reality, if you care about the issues that affect your life as a woman, then you are a feminist. But, if the label offends you, forget about it. Don't let it deter you from getting involved and taking a position. "That word has taken such a beating. The language is attacked—not so much the underlying concept," said First Lady Hillary Rodham Clinton.[2]

In terms of running for elective office, bias and prejudice often deter women. The attitude that a woman's place is in the home results from a society that frowns upon a woman with small children running for office. Remember, when Congresswoman Mary Bono, Sony Bono's widow, decided to run for his congressional seat after his tragic and untimely death, her mother-in-law openly criticized her because of the time the job would take away from her children.

"No one would say anything if the man did that because you would assume that he had someone taking care of the children—the wife. Whereas if a woman decides to go get elected and has small children, she may be criticized. So most women will wait until their children are well established in school before they will take on a major campaign for office," said Harriett Woods, former lieutenant governor from the State of Missouri and past president of the National Women's Political Caucus.

Finally, women who run for elective office not only face prejudice from male voters but may find that other women abandon them. Women must be willing to support women candidates. That seems like an obvious statement, but many women who have run for public office say women were much more critical of them than men were.

Take Michela Alioto, for example, who ran for Congress in California at the age of twenty-seven. She won her party's primary by a substantial margin, but without any endorsements from women's organizations.

"I was told by my consultant that I'd get the women's vote, and that was absolutely a wrong conclusion to make. It's the opposite. Women are tougher on women. In part, I think they want to make sure that when they elect a female to office, they're electing somebody [who] represents their gender. So women would be much more likely not to vote for a female because they don't represent the way they want the female gender to be represented," she said.

Women candidates need your vote. "When women vote, women win," said EMILY's List president, Ellen Malcolm. Women's votes have made a significant difference in the outcome of a number of elections during the past decade. For political strategists, the 1996 presidential race served as a primer on the impact of women's votes. Among male voters, Clinton and Dole broke even, but women ushered Clinton back into the White House with a 16 percent lead over Dole. This phenomenon has now been labeled the gender gap, and as a result, current-day political agendas are packed with messages that address the issues that score highly with women and attract women voters.

Your vote counts. Don't take for granted your hard-won right of franchise. It is your voice in government and how you hold your elected officials accountable.

"Let's face it, women—who earn about seventy-five cents for every dollar earned by men—cannot go dollar-for-dollar against Ross Perot, Donald Trump, or George W. Bush. If you don't believe me, just ask Elizabeth Dole. However, when we combine all of our resources—our money, our volunteer time, and our votes—we can, and do, make the difference in elections," said Patricia Ireland, president of the National Organization for Women (NOW).[3]

We Need a Woman's Voice

"If they [women] all got together on the same day, in the same state of mind, they could radically alter life in America simply by pulling voting levers."

—Sherrye Henry, *Deep Divide—Why Women Resist Equality*

We need women in positions of public policy–making who can be advocates for our rights. We need women whose life experiences parallel our own. Researchers note there are frequently large gaps in the opinions and actions of male and female legislators, particularly on issues important to women, such as education, the environment, health care, and domestic violence.

"One thing that I think is really important is that women have a seat at the table. You will definitely change the tone of the conversation when you introduce a woman to the process. She will bring a different tone, a different strategy, and a different outcome to the process. She can take that power and use it to her advantage and it will be beneficial for everyone," explained Terry Neese.

"The Senate right now is 91 percent guys. Some of them are very good guys who carry issues of equality and fairness, but they have a different experience in life. I would like to have at the table people who get pregnant, people who have experience in domestic violence, people who have been on public assistance, people who have awakened in the middle of the night and tried to figure out how to get medical care for their child because the government has cut

Medicaid and Medicare and is about to cut Social Security,"[4] stated Patricia Ireland during a public debate at McKendree College in November 1999.

Marie Wilson is the driving force behind The White House Project, a nonpartisan group with the goal of electing a woman president in ten years, and she has said, "Women do bring private concerns into the public arena. How do children and the elderly get taken care of, how can work and family get dealt with, the whole business of equity? What can we bring to the table?"[5]

In addition to legislative advocacy, women elected officials are more likely to place more women in key appointed positions, such as judgeships, agency heads, and on governmental boards and commissions. Such appointments broaden the opportunity for women to shape public policy and influence the events that shape our lives.

Diversity in government strengthens the democratic process. "If we're going to have a government that is truly representative of the populace, then it needs to represent every age and every group," said Michela Alioto.

Finding Your Role in the Process

Start with issues you are passionate about. Women usually are motivated to get into public service because there is a problem they see and they want to solve it. It doesn't necessarily have to be a political issue. Harriett Woods, the former lieutenant governor of the State of Missouri and past president of the National Women's Political Caucus, became involved in politics because of the traffic in her neighborhood. She was a young mother who liked to get a little respite in the afternoon when her three children—three little boys under the age of four—were down for naps. On the street, just outside the boys' bedroom window, was a loose manhole cover. "It seemed every time the boys got their heads down, some car would hit that loose manhole cover and at least one of the kids would wake up," she explained.

Furious, Woods went to the governing body in her community and demanded that either the traffic be stopped or they fix the manhole cover. "They just sort of stared at me. So I did what women were doing all over the country at the time, and I took a yellow legal pad and a pen and went door to door and got signatures. And magically there was a response," she said.

From that moment on, Woods learned that numbers make a difference, and people began to look at her as a leader. "If you have an idea you believe in and can get others to follow, you can get something done. And so, it wasn't that in itself that automatically made me a politician, but it gave me a sense that I could be someone who was part of the solution instead of part of the problem," she continued.

You too can be an important part of the solution, when you make the decision to get involved. Stay informed about the issues that affect you as a woman and those that impact your community. It is important to be well-informed because when you are armed with the pertinent facts, you will have more confidence to speak up and state your opinion. Others will begin to look to you as a spokesperson.

Get to know the candidates for office as well as your elected officials. Learn where they stand on issues that are important to you.

"When one of our former mayors in Oklahoma City was running for office, he says I called him up and said I wanted to interview him. I told him I'd decide after I interviewed him whether or not I'd support him. I don't really remember doing this, but according to his story, I came over and interviewed him and made the decision on the spot that I wanted to support him. You see surveys show that women are believable to the American public. They trust us. It means a great deal to a candidate for a credible woman or a credible small business owner to be supporting them. One person can make a huge difference in the race. Then, when the candidate wins you obviously have access to the candidate, you know the candidate well. Those are things that I think we have to do as community leaders and particularly as small business owners. I call it 'GIPOGOOB'—Get Involved Politically Or Go Out Of Business," explained Terry Neese.

Get out Your Checkbook

"It has always been a man's game, and it will continue to be a man's game until women are willing to step up and put their money where their mouths are."

—Georgette Mosbacher, author of *It Takes Money, Honey*

Money is the driving force behind successful political campaigns. Only the most naive would think someone could win an election today without adequate campaign financing. One of the biggest difficulties for women candidates is raising the money they need to be considered viable. The level of financial support has not kept pace with the number of women entering the political arena. Women make up only 25 percent of all campaign donors.[6]

"Women haven't been writing checks. They haven't been contributing dollars, and that has really been a deficit," said Edie Fraser, president of the Business Women's Network.

When commenting on Elizabeth Dole's bid for the Republican presidential nomination, former Representative Pat Schroeder said, "She's going to need to bring in $100,000 a day to be competitive, and they don't give you a discount because you're a woman."[7]

Ultimately, it was a lack of funding that sank Elizabeth Dole's campaign. During an interview with NBC news on October 21, 1999, the day after she announced her decision to withdraw from the race, she explained that it is still hard for women to raise money. The good ole boy network of the Republican party was not going to finance Elizabeth Dole's campaign, so she focused her efforts on nontraditional funding sources. She pulled thousands of women into the political process—women who had never been involved in a campaign effort before. Personally, I was tapped to serve on a local fund-raising committee in St. Louis that was comprised entirely of other businesswomen—most of whom had never been involved with political fundraising. However, Elizabeth Dole closed up shop on her historic bid to become the Republican candidate for the presidency in 2000 because she could not raise enough money. Even after seventy fund-raising events across the country, George W. Bush still had a cash advantage of seventy-five to one.

"I hoped to compensate by attracting new people to the political process, by emphasizing experience and advocating substantive issues. But as important as these things may be, the bottom line remains money. In fact, it's a kind of Catch 22. Inadequate funding limits the number of staff at headquarters and in key states. It restricts your ability to communicate with voters. It places a ceiling on travel and travel staff. Over time, it becomes nearly impossible to sustain an effective campaign," Dole explained in a widely distributed campaign e-mail dated October 25, 1999.

Undoubtedly, Elizabeth Dole's campaign helped to pave the way for future women presidential candidates. However, if women are not willing to put their money where their mouth is, it will be difficult for a woman to actually win an elective office.

"Women can raise as much money as men for comparable races. But I don't care whether it's a woman or a man, it's very hard to raise money when you're a newcomer. But women can do it, they may raise it differently from different sources. When I ran for the United States Senate in 1982 against Missouri Senator Jack Danforth, it was very hard for us to raise money because I was the challenger to a well-financed, well-known incumbent. I think we finally raised in both the primary and general about a million and a quarter. And a lot of it was reaching out to women who were just beginning to move in the 1980s into business and professional careers. Our goal was to find a hundred women to give a thousand dollars each, even if they did it in the installment plan. When I ran for the Senate in 1986, I was an established politician, I was lieutenant governor, and it was much easier to raise money. I raised about four million for that campaign," Harriett Woods explained.

"While I detest the money flow into politics and what it does, we have to understand that money is where it is at. We can't write a check for $100 or $200. What I encourage women to do is to look at themselves and write down what they have on. If I'm at a fundraising event, then I would say to a person, look at your shoes, your hose, the dress you have on, your coat, your jewelry, your makeup, your scarf—add it all up, and what did you pay for those items? Add it up and write a check for that amount," said Terry Neese.

Neese makes a strong point when it comes to contributions. We are talking about an opportunity to shape and mold public policy and the laws that impact our personal and professional lives. We are talking about power. Isn't your future worth the cost of a new outfit?

Building a Bridge

Despite the disproportionate representation numbers that exist today, women are beginning to make some significant strides in the political arena. In January 1999, Arizona became the first state with an all-female line of succession. Its new governor, secretary of state, attorney general, treasurer, and schools chief are all women.

We can build a bridge to close the gap by getting involved in the process, voting, and making financial contributions. But in addition, we must provide additional training and support for potential women candidates.

"There really needs to be someone who can step up to the plate, that can really do a lot of training and education with women who want to run for office. It is extremely difficult. I ran for lieutenant governor in 1990, and I only lost by about six thousand votes, but I can tell you that it's extremely difficult. There needs to be more education and training for women candidates," explained Terry Neese.

Currently, organizations like the League of Women Voters play instrumental roles in providing hands-on training. Through workshops, seminars, and training manuals, potential women candidates learn how to conduct winning campaigns. Also, Yale University offers a four-and-a-half-day comprehensive training session for potential women candidates that are taught by leading political strategists. To learn more about these programs, visit the league's Web site at www.lwv.org.

Training and education are important because women have not historically been groomed to run for public office. Additionally, because of past discrimination in terms of educational and career opportunities, women have not been considered as qualified to run for office as men. So women have had to overcome this hurdle and shore up their qualifications to be accepted as good candidates. Therefore, as successful businesswomen, we not only need to get involved in the process ourselves but to encourage young women as well. Politics should be positioned as a legitimate career path for women.

"I think we need to start talking to women back in high school. [W]e need to start talking to our young girls about running for office and about making this not only a viable option for them but an ordinary one, and one that they think of. You know the normal path of young men is to do stuff like this. We need to make it an ordinary path for young women who are interested in politics also and [to] run for office and to do something like that," said Michela Alioto.

Notes

1. Mae C. Jemison and Claudia Kennedy, "Electoral Revolution Needs a Bigger Army: Women Have to Run in Larger Numbers," *Monitor*, July 2, 1999.
2. Calvin Woodward, "A Century of Women's Progress Noted," www.womenconnect.com, March 17, 1999.
3. Patricia Ireland, NOW president, "Women Will Decide the 2000 Elections," www.ivillage.com, February 18, 2000.
4. Taken from a debate between Patricia Ireland, NOW president, and Phyllis Schafley, president of The Eagle Forum, McKendree College, Lebanon, Ill., November 10, 1999.
5. Ellen Goodman, "The Ms. President Project," *Washington Post*, September 26, 1998.
6. Ibid., p. 51.
7. "Quotes of the Year: The Best and Worst of 1999," *Toledo Blade*, www.womenconnect.com/linkto/12231999_wcmm.htm, December 23, 1999.

THE POWER OF MONEY

"An old Chinese proverb says 'women hold up half the sky.' It will be a lot easier to hold up our half if we own the ground we're standing on."

—**Ronnie Feit, attorney and consultant**

Once upon a time, there was a beautiful young maiden who was sitting in her garden admiring the lovely flowers. Suddenly, a frog jumped up and sat down beside her. The frog said, "Beautiful young maiden, an evil witch has cast a spell on me. I am actually a handsome prince who lives in a beautiful castle. If you will kiss me and break the spell, I will marry you and we will live happily ever after in my palace where you can wait on me, cook for me, clean for me, and bear my children."

Later that evening, as the beautiful young maiden sat sipping a glass of the finest champagne and enjoying a gourmet meal of frog legs sautéed in white wine, she thought to herself, "No way, sucker."

A friend e-mailed this parody of a favorite childhood fairy tale to me, and I found it humorous, and at the same time telling. Through sarcastic wit, it attacks the foundation upon which many women develop their attitudes toward money. Girls are brought up to believe in fairy tales where a Prince Charming gallantly cares for her forever and ever. And they live happily ever after. The end.

Once upon a time, it wasn't considered feminine for beautiful young maidens to think about money. Whether explicitly stated or fictionally illustrated, the message was loud and clear—there is no need to worry your pretty little head about money.

Unfortunately, the real world is not a fairy tale and as for living happily ever after—forget about it. You are not Cinderella. There is no Prince Charming. You, and only you, are responsible for your financial well-being. Allowing yourself to end up in a financially dependent situation is just plain stupid.

As an attorney, I've seen countless numbers of women become destitute or reliant upon family members because of the untimely death of a spouse. Did you know the average age of widowhood in this country is fifty-five to fifty-seven, and the vast majority of these women are living in poverty? That should wake you up.

I have also sadly seen far too many women trapped in unhappy and abusive relationships because of economic dependence. Women who have been full-time homemakers and have no marketable skills find themselves with no means to support themselves or their children should they decide to leave. So they bravely (or foolishly) look the other way when it comes to infidelity, they make excuses for drunkenness, and they cover up abuse. Eventually, their self-esteem slips away, and all that remains is a shell of a human being.

Take the story of Joann. Joann packed up her three children in the middle of the night, with only the clothes on their backs, and fled an abusive marriage. Unable to find work, Joann and the kids were homeless for nine months and forced to eat out of trash cans. A strong faith kept Joann going, and slowly she pulled herself out of poverty. Joann entered a welfare-to-work program, where she received the training and financial assistance needed to start a lawn-care business. One year later, she was earning enough money to move her family into a small house. In an interview with Joann, I asked her what kept her from giving up. She told me she stopped believing all the bad things people said, and started believing the good. She is truly an inspiration.

However, her story is an example of the struggles women face because of economic inequities—and for every Joann, there are hundreds of stories without happy endings. Women make up three-fifths of all people living in poverty in the United States.[1] The reality is that, at some point, the majority of women in this country will find themselves solely responsible for their own financial security. That is why you need to start planning your financial future now, no matter what your current circumstances are. It is naive to think that it won't happen to you—particularly if you have your head in the clouds, living in happily married bliss. You never know what tomorrow will bring.

Take, for instance, a young family I know. The father was a carpenter, his wife did not work, and they had three young children. He was the picture of health in his early thirties. One Saturday afternoon, he went to lie down with a headache. Later that day, he was found dead—the victim of a massive aneurysm. He and his wife had done no financial planning, and they had very little savings. Lacking job skills, his widow found herself relying on the charity of friends and family to support herself and her three children. It could happen to any one of us at any time.

Furthermore, as we all know, over half the marriages in this country end in divorce. In 1999, 2.2 million Americans exchanged marriage vows, while 1.1 million wound up divorced. And divorce results in a drop in the standard of living for most women. Alimony, once a nearly automatic cushion for women, is now practically unheard of in the majority of states. Only 15 percent of divorced women get any type of court-ordered spousal support, and then 5 percent of that number get nothing.[2] As for child support, it is usually inadequate and many divorced fathers don't bother to pay it. Some of the fathers that I have represented resented having to pay more than the bare minimum in child support. That situation always perplexed me because, after all, they are the children of these men. But that is the way the system works.

"Women have really been screwed by the so-called divorce laws—especially the women who have stayed home for twenty years as part of a partnership agreement with their husbands [so] that they would take care of the family and the home while [the] husband would bring home the money and advance his career. These women are ending up in poverty after a divorce and men are ending up wealthier. These women have salaries that just cover themselves, and child support payments are usually inadequate to cover the children's needs. These women should also be receiving alimony because of the partnership agreement, but they are not," said Claudia Wayne, former director of the National Pay Equity Commission.

According to financial expert and founder of Envestnet.com Mary Lehman MacLachlan, the concept of honor and obey in the traditional marriage ceremony creates a cultural bias that teaches women to wait for some man to take over their lives. Therefore, they do not make strategic plans for themselves.

"If I said to you, you have to go to the dentist a couple of times a year to have your teeth checked, you'd know that it is your responsibility to take care of that. You wouldn't wait for some man to tell you it's time to go to the dentist. But, if I said [that] you need to review your insurance policy, investment strategy, and liability situation once a year, most women wouldn't think of that as their responsibility. It's not in their lexicon. But when you ask them whose responsibility it is, you get all sorts of answers," MacLachlan explained.

It is every woman's responsibility to take control of her financial future for herself and for the well-being of her family. "No matter how much society might prefer to keep women dependent, they must make the voyage of life alone; and for safety in case of emergency, they must know something of the laws of navigation,"[3] said early feminist leader Elizabeth Cady Stanton at an 1892 women's convention.

When it comes to financial matters, women definitely need to know the laws of navigation. Yet, the majority of women choose to be passive observers. Over one-third of the women in this country do absolutely no financial planning. For your own personal welfare, as well as your family's, it is imperative that you understand the importance of economic independence and how to get there. That is the only way to stop the cycle of financial dependency that keeps women chained to second-class citizenry.

Women Start off from a Weak Position

Earlier I discussed the issue of pay equity for women. We know that women earn less than their male counterparts do. Yet, the wage gap is more extensive than it may initially appear because it jeopardizes not only your current financial situation but also severely impacts your family's well-being and your future financial security.

According to an AFL-CIO survey, women who work full-time are paid on average $148 less per week. In terms of a dual-income family, the survey found that working families lose a staggering $200 billion of income annually to the wage gap, an average loss of more than $4,000 each. Additionally, single working mothers' incomes would rise 13.4 percent if they earned as much as men.[4]

Even though women earn less than men, their cost of living expenses remain the same. Housing, cars, insurance, clothing, and food are not discounted proportionally. That means women have less discretionary income to save and invest, which cripples their future financial security. Because women earn less and concomitantly pay in less, they will receive lower social security benefits when they retire. Additionally, the value of any employer-sponsored retirement plan will be less. Ironically, while women's retirement benefits will be far less than men's, in all likelihood, they will live longer.

"Women who don't prepare themselves financially are practically guaranteeing they'll be a burden on someone—most likely their husband or their children," said Mary Lehman MacLachlan.

Viewing the wage gap in broader terms drives home the necessity for women to insist on pay equity. The federal government recently stepped up its efforts to remedy the wage gap. The Department of Labor began an aggressive campaign to eliminate the gender wage gap by stepping up its enforcement of pay discrimination laws. Companies like Texaco, Xerox, and CoreStates Financial were ordered to increase the salaries of female employees. For example, Texaco, in a $3.1 million settlement, agreed to pay 186 female employees back pay ranging from $1,700 to $51,000 for the three-year period covered by the department's audit.

Regulatory oversight is important, but on an individual level, you have a duty to ensure that you earn what you are worth. To combat the gender bias in wages, women must know their market value and be prepared to fight for it. Because most women's salaries currently lag behind those of men, when they change jobs or get promoted, they usually get offered less than a man would for the same work. Salary offers are based on a formula that begins with your current salary level.

"Let me give you an example. If you have a job opening that pays between $80,000 to $125,000, someone coming in making $100,000 will probably be offered the $125,000. However, if a woman comes in who is currently making $75,000, they aren't going to necessarily offer her $125,000. Most new jobs or promotional increases are based on what you're currently earning, or what it's going to take to get the person you really need or want," explained Eric Segal, COO of Kenzer Corporation, an executive recruiting firm.

Therefore, women in the past have started off from a weaker negotiating standpoint. There is also a prevailing attitude that women don't need to earn as much because they are not the primary breadwinner in their families. One of my former bosses at ITT said to me, "Well, you don't really have to work. Your husband makes a lot of money." You should have seen the expression on his face when I explained my husband (now ex-husband) didn't really have a job, and that I was the primary breadwinner in my household.

"I have to admit there are some issues that come up where some companies tend to view the role of a male as the breadwinner. The guy who has the family at home to support and, therefore, they have to bend a little bit more to help him. Then they see the female employee as someone who probably is a single, hardheaded, hard-charging female, with a point to prove and accomplishments to gain. It's getting better, but it's not 100 percent correct yet," said Segal.

Show Me the Money

The first step toward ensuring that you are not underearning is to become comfortable talking about money and asking for what you are worth. Women can easily get shortchanged when it comes to salaries or pricing their services because they shy away from the topic of money. We will openly discuss intimate details about our personal relationships, our sex lives, and our deepest fears and insecurities. But heaven forbid that we talk openly about money. The topic is considered off limits. Some of the most successful women whom I have interviewed candidly admitted that they aren't comfortable asking for money.

"I think women need to learn how to negotiate better. I think we are going to have a harder time than the men because the employer is willing to hire the mediocre man at $40,000 and is expecting to hire the skilled woman at $30,000. The negotiations are therefore harder. In addition, women have been socialized [to believe] that it is not polite to talk about money and it is not polite to be in confrontations. As a result of these factors and discrimination, women can be taken advantage of tremendously in the workplace," said Claudia Wayne.

"As a business owner, I have problems talking about money,

particularly when it comes to setting firm terms with my clients and when it comes to collections. I'm getting better about it, but it's still something that I don't feel totally comfortable with," said Iris Salsman, a principal in the public relations firm Salsman Lundgren.

Jane Applegate, CEO and founder of SBTV.com, solved the problem of asking for money by hiring someone to represent her. "I learned from the beginning you always do better in a negotiation when somebody else speaks for you. So when someone asks me what my fees are, or what something costs, we provide some basic information, but I think it's important to have somebody on your team [who] will get into all the details of the deal. I think you can always get more money that way," she explained.

Companies are always looking at the bottom line. Therefore, if they can get away with paying you less or taking longer to pay you, they will because it is good for their profitability. To get what you deserve, you must know your market value. When I make that statement, most women ask me, "Well how do I know that?"

To determine your economic value, consider the market rate for your position in the industry, not just your particular company. Factor in your personal performance and special skills. The same is true if you are a business owner. Find out how your competitors are pricing their products or services. You don't want to be the lowest or the highest price—you want to be the right price.

Obtaining this information is not as difficult as you may think. Keep your ear close to the ground. You may pick up useful information from bits and pieces of casual conversation at the coffee machine or at a cocktail party. Of course, you can always ask one of your business associates. He or she may or may not be willing to share specifics but perhaps will give you a salary range. Additionally, there are industrywide salary surveys and statistics on pricing available at the public library or in trade publications. Trade associations can often be good sources, as well. Annually, *Working Woman* magazine conducts a comprehensive salary survey of various professions, which can give you a basis for comparison. The Department of Labor publishes statistics by job category. You can also do research on the Internet by using the key words *salary survey*.

Executive recruiters can be a tremendous resource in helping you establish your market value. You should develop a relationship with a headhunter or recruiter whom you can call for counsel. These professionals keep their fingers on the pulse of the market and can provide fairly accurate ranges based on your personal skills and experience. You should get as much data as possible. Do not rely on one piece of information. Do thorough research so that you will feel confident asking for the rate you deserve.

"It's no different than talking to an accountant about getting the best tax advice, talking to a lawyer for the best legal advice. So why not talk to a headhunter who works with your industry, understands the industry, and will look to grow a relationship with you and be able to be there for career advice," said Eric Segal.

Compensation consultant Christy Martin says that it is important to know what you want and to ask a lot of questions. "Find out what a company's pay philosophy is, and how they compare to the market. Do they see employees as a cost or an investment? Find out what the salary range is for the particular job. Often, salary ranges are divided into quartiles so you'll want to know what it takes to be in each one of those. Try to start as close to the middle of that range as possible. Don't forget to factor in the supply and demand for your job. If the supply is small and demand is larger, you can push farther into the range. Ask about bonus programs and incentive programs, and any other aspects of the job which you value," she explained.

Additionally, Martin advises avoiding the inclination to deflate your value or your price. Do not be timid to answer confidently when a prospect asks you how much money you want. This question can make your stomach turn, your heart race, and your palms sweat, but if you have done your homework, you can answer confidently. Keep in mind that just because you ask for it, you might not always get what you want. However, I guarantee that you will gain respect because you know what you are worth.

Money Means Power and Freedom

"Money can't buy happiness, but it can make you a lot more comfortable in your misery."

—Susan Solovic

There's an old expression that money is the root of all evil. Well, it can be, but if you remember from whence it came and how quickly it can be taken away, and you use a portion of it to do good, then all the rest falls in place. There is no other way to describe it, money gives you freedom in every way you can think," said Barb Gilman, partner in the brokerage firm Edward Jones.

Taking care of your financial fitness is as important as taking care of your physical fitness. When you are financially secure, no one can tell you what you can and cannot do, and that is important. Money gives you choices. Not only is that true in terms of relationships, but also in terms of careers. If you carefully plan your financial future, you will have more flexibility in making career decisions. You won't live in fear of being downsized. You will be prepared for emergencies. Plus, a stash of cash is critical if you want to start your own business.

"It always floors me when I hear somebody say, 'Well, my husband won't let me do that.' *Let* is not a part of my marital vocabulary. There is an unspoken message that if you don't have the financial control to do what you want to do, then you are in a weaker position," said Iris Salsman.

Marsha Serlin, the multimillion-dollar scrap metal maven, believes that, to some degree, she has to thank her ex-husband for making her successful. She says that if he had given her any of the money he promised her in court, she wouldn't have started her own business and been so successful. Economic necessity precipitated her entrepreneurial endeavors. "You know while money isn't everything, it's a reward. And if you're not going to work to make money, then why do it. I've enjoyed the financial freedom, and I've been able to buy a lovely home, which I enjoy and I travel a lot too. But the best part is while I am in a relationship now, I don't need anybody to take care of me. I like to invite people into my life and that's fine. But I can completely take care of myself, and that's a wonderful feeling," she said.

Successful women realize that economic independence means freedom. Their primary goal is not always to make a lot of money, but it is an important means to an end. "Women are essential to the financial health of America. And I think what women have to do is get a sense of entitlement, to stand up and demand things for themselves. I don't mean burning bras, but I think women still don't understand how to say 'I want that salary because I deserve it,' or that 'I want to be rich.' There is nothing wrong with wanting to be rich," explained Mary Lehman MacLachlan.

No Excuses—Do It

M any women don't feel comfortable with financial matters. It is the fear of math phenomenon. We fall back on the "I'm no good with numbers" excuse to avoid the subject. Investing in our company's 401(k) plan, establishing a college savings fund, or dabbling with a few stock purchases is usually the extent of our financial planning. "It always amazes me when you meet very successful women and they say, 'Oh, my husband manages the investing or finances,' and I can't imagine that they wouldn't want to know everything about it. After all, it's their money, too," said Flori Roberts, founder of Flori Roberts Cosmetics and a member of the Committee of 2000.

During her tenure at U.S. Trust Company as head of the estate planning and financial counseling department, Mary Lehman MacLachlan became interested in the topic of women as investors. She began doing seminars for women because she witnessed a complete abdication of responsibility.

"When I would do financial counseling for a corporate executive, I would encourage him to bring his wife into the process, and the wife was almost always passive and not knowledgeable or interested. A lot of times the issues for the husband would evolve around who is going to take care of my wife if something happens to me.

There were wives who didn't know how to write checks and that was unbelievable. So I started teaching seminars back in the 1980s trying to teach women the basics of money, not even investing," Mary Lehman MacLachlan explained.

MacLachlan says that women of all ages are not thinking strategically about money. "Because there will come a time when every woman will be alone, how can she not think strategically about this? If women would plan for themselves in the same way they plan for their children, they'd get there," she said.

Whatever excuse you've used in the past to put off planning for your personal wealth and security, now is the time to start. You must educate yourself on the basics. You may not have learned it growing up, but you're a smart, sophisticated woman and financial savvy is imperative for success and power.

Take a seminar on investing, or better yet, enroll in a full-blown financial class at a local college. You may also enjoy becoming part of an investment club, where you can learn about investing—and you might make a little money in the process. An interesting side note is that, on average, womens' investment clubs outperform all-male investment clubs. In 1999, it was by an average of 10 percent better returns.[5] If you are interested in learning more about investment clubs, you can contact The National Association of Investment Clubs at 248-583-6242.

Afraid you might look like a dope? Turn to the Internet. The Internet has a plethora of information about investing and financial issues; in fact, it can be overwhelming. Be careful. Not all the information you find on the Internet is reliable. Go with names you know, such as *The Wall Street Journal*'s Web site or the one for Dow Jones University. Be selective.

Take time to read the business and financial section of your local newspaper or subscribe to a publication like *The Wall Street Journal*. Some of the business news channels like CNBC or CNN/fn are great resources, too. There are also some excellent books on investing. One of my favorites is *One Up on Wall Street* by Warren Buffet.

The bottom line is to stop making excuses. Make a commitment to yourself that you are going to learn more about, and get comfortable with, the subject of money. Your personal finances and your business financial picture will benefit tremendously.

Be Selfish—Pay Yourself First

Wishful thinking won't create a secure financial future. Building your financial freedom takes hard work and planning, just like anything else. In order to succeed, you must evaluate your current financial situation. Take time to examine your personal values about money. Determine what your financial goals are; then create a workable plan.

You don't have to have a lot of money to invest to set off on the road to financial security. Many of the mutual fund companies allow you to open an account with as little as $250 and a monthly investment of $25. In this economy, before you know it, the dollars really start adding up. And let's face it, $25 a month isn't a lot of money. Cut out a couple of trips to the movie theater or a Friday night dinner out and you're there. "The key, however, is to remember to pay yourself first. Don't wait to see if there is anything left over because there never is enough to go around.

"Even if you are happily living in a traditional marriage where you get money to run the household and your husband manages the rest, you can always take five or ten dollars off the top and put it in an account. I'm not suggesting you be clandestine about it, but it's important to start the savings process. Before long you'll have enough money to make a meaningful investment. But it all starts with paying yourself first, and most people don't do that," added Gilman.

As a first-time investor, choosing the right investment can be intimidating. You should find a good financial adviser who can assist you. Shop around and get references from people whose opinions you trust. A financial adviser can help you create a sound financial plan based on your personal goals and economic circumstances. But you should be comfortable with your adviser. Meet with him or her and make certain that it is someone who will listen to your concerns and patiently answer your questions. Run as fast as you can from those who say, "Trust me honey, I'll take care of you." After all, it is your money and you have the right to make well-informed decisions.

The Internet can be a resource for financial-planning advice, too. Mary Lehman MacLachlan recently launched Envestnet.com, which provides a whole wealth management network to independent financial advisers. As a potential investor, you can go to the Web site and provide financial information by filling out a planning questionnaire. Once you have provided the necessary information, you will receive help in determining what your goals are and how to reach them.

"Then, we'll look at your situation and determine where your assets should be allocated. Asset allocation is something people always say they don't understand, but everybody has it, even if it's by default. But we'll teach you about it. You'll work with a planner, and we'll monitor your assets for you. And you can go online every day and see the full picture of your portfolio," MacLachlan explained.

There is no legitimate reason for not taking responsibility for your own financial well-being. So forget the fairy tales and take responsibility for yourself. Economic independence means freedom of choice and it means power—power over your own life, power to care for your family, and power to create change. Without this power, equal status for women cannot be achieved.

Notes

1. Taken from a 1999 Center for Policy Alternatives publication, "America's Economic Agenda: Women's Voices for Solutions. Blueprint for Action," p. 4.
2. Anne Letterese, "Women and Retirement Wake-Up Call! Invasion of the Grannybabies," www.fool.com, June 12, 2000.
3. Patricia Edmonds, "Not for Ourselves Alone: Elizabeth Cady Stanton, Su-

san B. Anthony and the Quest for Women's Rights," www.womencon nect.com, November 5, 1999.

4. Taken from a survey, "Equal Pay for Working Families: National and State Data," www.aflcio.org/women/exec99.htm, January 23, 2000.

5. Jean Sherman Chatzky, "Real-Life Guide to Investing," www.money .com, May 1, 2000.

A VISION FOR THE FUTURE

"Ultimately, to get to equality, it's women who will have to lead the way. It's not going to be handed to us. If we've learned one thing, nothing will be gained without a real, intense struggle."

—Elenaor Smeal, president of the Feminist Majority

A Feminine World

In December 1919, *Forbes* magazine published an article entitled "How Girls Can Succeed in Business," which stated: "The big difference between young men and women in business is that the former know they have many years of work ahead, while the latter often feel that their sojourn in the business world is to be temporary. Only to the extent that a girl considers her work as a lifetime affair, and accordingly devotes her whole heart and soul to it, can she succeed in rising above the rank and file."[1]

The inference in this article is that a "girl's" devotion to her career meant forgoing marriage and family. After all, most of us grew up hearing the message that a woman's real place is in the home. Yet, women have been devoting their hearts and souls to their careers for decades, only today they do so without sacrificing a family life. But there continues to be a prejudice against women, who are often seen as less serious about their careers because of their domestic responsibilities.

About ten years ago, driven by the sheer number of women in the workforce, businesses recognized the need to begin to examine work/family issues. Male executives cleverly crafted the "mommy track," ostensibly to accommodate working mothers. In reality, the mommy track was a sidetrack that derailed women's careers. Even more troubling was the fact that the impact of career and family was seen as a women's issue, involving nothing more than child care.

> *"We, along with other Western societies, are unique in the exclusiveness of the mother's role as infant caretaker and in our emphasis on her importance in the development of a child's attachments."*
>
> —Margaret Mead, anthropologist

When women allow businesses to make work and family a so-called women's issue, we are ratifying and perpetuating narrow-minded attitudes about the proper role of women and our commitment to our professional lives. Work/family issues are broad and comprehensive, involving not only mothers and children but fathers and their children, aging parents, and quality-of-life concerns. Society must evolve to reflect a gender-neutral attitude toward these issues. In the future, a new business paradigm needs to emerge that depicts the realities of the modern-day workforce. Women will have to lead the way.

Those of us who grew up in the 1950s and 1960s remember

the idealistic message of television programs like *Leave It to Beaver*. Ward Cleaver went to work every day in his suit and tie, while June happily went about her household chores wearing a full-skirted dress and pearls. Today, only 13 percent of all families fit this traditional model of husband as wage earner and wife as homemaker.[2] According to the U.S. Bureau of Labor Statistics, more than 60 percent of all marriages are dual-career marriages, making up 45 percent of the working population and representing the largest single group of families in the workforce.[3]

"It's an economic issue, and that's becoming clearer and clearer. The old prototype of an employee who has a stay-at-home spouse, which allows them to work endless hours, is over. And it's not just women who are coming into the workforce that are changing that dynamic, it's the men, too," said Vanessa Freytag, president of W-Insight, Inc. "You have to have two incomes to achieve the same lifestyles that your parents could achieve with one. Whether companies like it or not, they are going to have to change."

Working wives contribute substantially to family incomes. In 1997, the median income for married couples with the wife in the paid labor force was $60,669, compared with $36,027 for those without the wife in the paid labor force. While helping to ease economic burdens for the family is important, 67 percent of married working women reported that they would continue to work even if there were no financial need to do so.[4] Women want personal fulfillment, which was the premise of Betty Friedan's controversial 1963 book, *The Feminine Mystique*. Friedan wrote about the feeling of worthlessness resulting from the acceptance of a designated role that requires a woman to be intellectually, economically, and emotionally reliant on her husband. Her predictions were slightly ahead of her time.

Men and Women Want the Same Things

When both the mother and father of a family work, each has to take on more responsibilities at home to compensate. Most successful women who have children say their husbands are actively involved with parenting.

"Women today are well educated, and they just aren't putting up with having to do it all. They're saying, 'You've got to share with me because these are our children, not just mine.' So you see more husbands staying home with the kids or taking off to take a child to the doctor. I've even heard some of the younger men say they're better at raising the family than their wives are," said Marsha Serlin, CEO of United Scrap Metal.

Studies show that men and women want the same things when it comes to balancing their work and their personal lives. They want flexibility in arranging their own day-to-day schedules, and the ability to successfully blend their home life and their work life, but that calls for innovative support from employers.[5] When Baxter Medical surveyed its employees, the company learned that 49 percent of men versus 39 percent of women employees were looking for a new job because of work/life conflicts.[6]

"*Working Woman* magazine each year at its work/life conference names the top one hundred companies. We have found in different studies that to be on this list can truly impact your recruiting capability by 2 to 5 percent. It reduces the attrition rate and can really impact millions of dollars against the bottom line. Work/life is a business imperative for retention and recruitment," said Edie Fraser, president of Business Women's Network. "This has everyone's attention. Even *Forbes* is having a big conference, and ten years ago you never would have seen that."

Elder care is another rapidly growing concern for working professionals. Millions of Americans are already dealing with elder care, and it is an issue that the business world must do a better job of addressing in the future in order to keep talented employees. One in five working parents today is part of what is called the "sandwich generation" because they are simultaneously raising children and caring for elderly parents. Studies indicate that the number of Americans acting as caregivers has tripled since 1987.[7] While women are more likely than men to be caregivers, an increasing number of men have parental responsibility. Nearly half of employed caregivers report taking time off, coming in late, or working fewer hours, while 6 percent gave up work entirely due to care giving and 3.6 percent took early retirement.[8]

The new business paradigm recognizes that the need to balance work and family impacts both genders equally, which is an important step toward gender parity. When work/family issues are redefined in this manner, the hurtful, deeply rooted attitudes toward women are destroyed and women are allowed to achieve greater levels of success. Women want opportunities for professional and personal fulfillment. As First Lady Hillary Clinton said at the United National Fourth World Conference on Women in Beijing, China, on September 5, 1999, "If women have a chance to work and earn as full and equal partners in society, their families will flourish. And when families flourish, communities and nations will flourish."

Our Duty as Role Models for the Next Generation

Today, more and more women are successfully climbing the corporate ladder, launching multimillion dollar enterprises, and winning high-level political offices, which sends an important message to the next generation of women. These powerful women demonstrate that women are able to achieve in male-dominated venues, and they provide positive role models for young girls to emulate. However, the real message of equality and opportunity begins at home.

My mother was a pioneer—a successful woman entrepreneur, beginning in the late 1940s. Widowed at age twenty-nine during World War II, she returned to her hometown and opened a furniture store with her brother. She also became a partner in a savings and loan institution. Then, when she met and married my father, she sold her interest in both businesses and moved to the town where my father was employed as a funeral director. Not one to sit at home and do nothing, she launched "Wilson's Tot Shop," a retail clothing store for children that she quickly expanded to include women's clothing and dry goods. When I was five years old, my parents decided to open their own funeral home. Wilson Funeral Home enjoyed great success, and eventually my mother sold the clothing store to concentrate on the growing needs of the funeral business. My mother and father worked side by side until they sold the business and retired in their late seventies. I take great pride in my parents' accomplishments. They taught me important values about work and integrity. Furthermore, because my mother was an integral part of the business, it never occurred to me when I was growing up that mothers didn't work, and I never once felt cheated. Because I was raised in a home with two working parents, I grew up understanding that marriage is a partnership. For me, the idea of not working never crossed my mind. I always knew that I would work, and I always knew my husband would be a supportive partner.

When ABWA's Executive Director Carolyn Elman's two sons were young, she made the decision to return to work. She was intent on sending a message that there shouldn't be any reason why she would not work. "I think in many ways I forced my boys and my husband to deal directly with each other as opposed to having everything filtered through me. That was a really dramatic step in the way the relationships were going before I went back to work. Our arrangement was that my husband got the boys off to school, and I picked them up. I tried not to notice that some days they were wearing the same clothes three days in a row," she said.

Today, both of Elman's sons are adults and have their own careers and interests. But, she says she finds it interesting to watch how they interact with women. "It's especially interesting with the younger one, who has had a girlfriend for some time. They are very much equal. I took him shopping recently, and I suggested while we were out we pick up something for his girlfriend. He said he'd like to get her a new black cotton top because he had ruined hers when he did the laundry last week. But he said it in such a matter-of-fact way. It had been his turn to do the laundry. Male/female relationships are very different than they used to be," said Elman.

Children mimic what they see, and they emulate their parents. Therefore, when children grow up with a mother who has a career or runs a business and enjoys her own economic independence, traditional roles are redefined.

Karen Harriman, vice president of marketing and development for a regional health care organization, remembers an incident when her son was in grade school and he was upset because she couldn't be a room mother. Using simple language that her son could understand, Harriman explained to him what he would gain and what he would lose if she chose to quit her job. "I explained to him that if I left my job, it would give me time to become a room mother. But on the other hand, he would no longer get the opportunity to meet professional ballplayers like Todd Worrell or Tom Pagnozzi, because I would no longer be working with them. Plus, I pointed out the other fun trips and things we do because of my job. He thought about it, then told me he didn't want me to quit my job. After he put it in perspective, he realized that he received a lot of perks because his mom was a working mother," she explained.

"Children repeat the patterns that they see. If they have a mother who works, they will be more likely accepting of it and want it themselves and see the positive value of it. I know that both of my sons have girlfriends who are very professional women and would not want it any other way," explained Marsha Firestone, president of the Women Presidents' Organization.

"The good thing is that you're teaching your daughters a lesson that I think is important for them to learn, and you're actually showing it to them. And also, you're in a position of not just greater affluence, but you also have more experiences to share with them as they grow up and more things to give them," said Michela Alioto, who is a former member of Vice President Gore's domestic policy team.

In addition to being good role models, working mothers may also provide a biological benefit to their daughters. According to an article in the *New York Times*, working women have higher levels of testosterone than women who stay at home, and the daughters of working women have higher levels of testosterone than the daughters of housewives. Testosterone, the article noted, is correlated in both men and women with psychological dominance, confident physicality, and high self-esteem.[9]

Whether through biological or environmental methods, instead of indoctrinating the next generation with good-girl expectations and limitations, we must empower young women with the realization that success is skill-based and should not be defined by gender.

"I think girls and young women need to know they can be enormously successful, rich, and powerful because that lesson has historically only been given to boys. I work on a youth initiative now to promote entrepreneurship, and I love it. I want young girls to know they can own their own business[es]. They can definitely be anything they want to be. But you can't do it by just dreaming about it. I want to do my part to help lead the way for others, and mentoring has become a mission in my life," explained Flori Roberts, founder of Flori Roberts Cosmetics.

"Children are better off seeing a mother as a person who functions in the real world—in an adult world and not just as a caregiver. I've always worked. And a few years ago, my daughter, who was in college at the time, was the coxswain of her crewing team and she had a major problem with her boat and the coach. She came to me, not her father, with questions about how she should handle the situation. When people ask how can you not be at home teaching family values to your children, I say how can this not be more important? I taught her more about values than if I had been home baking cookies. I taught her about leadership and teamwork. And that whole interchange of her understanding that her mother is someone she could turn to about issues with the real world to me is a perfect example of how a woman who stays home in the house trying to teach her children values is missing half the boat. There are a lot of real values you don't know about in the real world if you stay at home," said Mary Lehman MacLachlan.

The good news is that young women have high expectations

for the future. According to a TIME/CNN survey, 50 percent of young women age eighteen to thirty-four said they share feminist values, by which they generally mean they want to live in a world where they can choose to be anything—the president of the United States, or a mother, or both. Now that is power.

Successful Women Speak about the Future

Legendary movie mogul Samuel Goldwyn once said, "Never make forecasts, especially about the future." Following this sage advice, I will refrain from making bold predictions about the future for women in business. However, I will say that these are exciting times for women. We are witnessing greater opportunities and experiencing more success than women, even a few decades ago, only dreamed of.

To reach the next echelon of success, it is going to take the right leadership and a commitment by all women. We must be instigators of change and strive to create a world where gender, age, race, and physical handicaps cease to be a defining factor. A world where no one is superior or inferior, but each of us is a valued participant, and we are judged individually on our abilities and not on traditional prejudices. It will take courage, perseverance, and commitment to change societal attitudes, but we are moving in the right direction. We can confidently look to the future with hope and inspired expectations.

"If all of our talents are available to solve the country's problems, if all of us have an opportunity to participate socially, politically, legally, will that not make for a better world?" asked Patricia Ireland, president of NOW, in a mass-distributed e-mail.

"It's a revolutionary period of time. I think [in] the next century we'll find the doors are totally wide open. There will be no limit on either the numbers of women in businesses or the kinds of businesses that women are running. In our middle generation we're sort of the pioneers, but I think our daughters and nieces and sisters are going to have a much easier time," said Jane Applegate, CEO and founder of SBTV.com.

"For the next generation, I hope there is now a level of understanding and acceptance for women, and while success is still skill-based, there will also be balance. I think that's vital. I know we used to talk about how you could have it all and be superwomen. Now, we know you can't have it all at the same time. And I always say it's all about having what you really want," said Vanessa Freytag.

"I think the playing field will level. I think that one of the great equalizers is business ownership because a woman can go out there and do well economically and in terms of gaining power and influence. As women gain more power, they make sure that other women who have more difficult problems will be addressed because it will finally be a women-led agenda," said Marsha Firestone.

"There really couldn't be a better time to be a woman. The economy is changing in so many ways—we need the female brain," said Helen Fisher, anthropologist and the author of *The First Sex: The Natural Talents of Women and How They Are Changing the World.*

"Twenty years ago, breaking down doors into the corporate world took center stage. In the last decade, breaking the glass ceiling became a major topic in the media. Though it feels like it's taking forever to change, it is happening. More specifically than that, young women's views of what's possible and acceptable are becoming much broader. I have a grown daughter, and she absolutely believes she can do anything and all will be available to her. She believes she has the choice of what she wants to do, not whether she can do it. I believe that when she has a daughter someday, my granddaughter may look at old pictures of heads of corporations and say, 'Oh, did men do those jobs back then?'" said Pamela Gilberd, author of *Eleven Commandments of Wildly Successful Women.*

Personally, I look at this new millennium as an empty canvas—a work in progress. My vision and hope is that books like this one will not be necessary at the turn of the next millennium because we will have created a masterpiece that depicts more harmony, peace, and equality in the world than we can begin to imagine today.

We all have important brush strokes to add to this masterpiece. In the powerful words of Helen Keller, "Alone we can do so little. Together we can do so much."

Notes

1. "Flashbacks," *Forbes*, October 4, 1999, p. 24.
2. "Facts on Working Women," U.S. Department of Labor, Women's Bureau, May 1998, No. 98-1.
3. Taken from a fact sheet on a Catalyst study of dual-career couples, "Two Careers, One Marriage: Making It Work in the Workplace," www.cata lystwomen.org/press/factsheet.html, August 23, 1999.
4. Ibid.
5. Ibid.
6. Mary Beth Grover, "Daddy Stress," *Forbes*, September 6, 2000, vol. 165, no. 5, p. 205.
7. "Eldercare Stress: A Dirty Little Secret among Working Women," www.womenCNNECT.com, August 25, 1999.
8. "Facts on Working Women," U.S. Department of Labor, Women's Bureau, May 1998, No. 98-1.
9. Andrew Sullivan, "The He Hormone," *New York Times*, April 2, 2000, p. 50.

ABWA (American Business Women's Association), 87
academia, 28
accommodation, as skill, 45–46
Albright, Madeline, 17, 40
Alioto, Michela
　on being a role model for your daughters, 195
　on need for education, 132
　on not being labeled, 128
　on women in politics, 166, 173
Alvarado, Linda, 31
Alverez, Alva, 17

American Business Women's Association (ABWA), 87
Anthony, Susan B., 164
Applegate, Jane
　on asking for money, 181
　on competition, 137–138
　on complacency, 113
　on mentors and mentoring, 118–120
　on not trying, 109
　on personal appearance, 67–68
　on present as revolutionary period, 197–198
　on taking time for herself, 158

Applegate, Jane (*continued*)
  on time management, 162
  on toxic people, 15
approachable, being, 91–92
assertive communication style, 60–61
Association of Women Brokers, 20
attitude(s)
  positive, 110–111
  societal, 2–10
Avon, 18–19

bad news, delivering, 59, 90
Baker, Bruce, on smiling by women, 74
Bennett, William, 94–95
Berner, Beverly
  on being ignored, 48
  on complacency, 112
  on emotional control, 97
  on not putting yourself down, 53
  on professional coaches, 122
  on quiet time, 158–159
  on saying you're sorry, 63
Berry, Kay
  on being one of the boys, 143
  on following her passion, 152–153
  on old boys network, 143
  on speaking up, 122
  on women in banking industry, 85
Bono, Sonny, 165
Bush, George W., 94–95, 171
business publications, writing for,
  106–107
business school, 11–12
"but" syndrome, 52–53

Calero, Kim, 29–30
  on dressing for business, 69
  on eye contact, 73
  on getting in the door, 84–85
  on nodding your head, 71
  on taking risks, 108
  on walking into a room, 70
career satisfaction, 7
Casperson, Dana May, 79
casual business attire, 69
Center for Creative Leadership, 19
charisma, 65–80
  and being positive, 77–78
  and creating a signature look, 67–69
  and creation of special connection,
    72–73
  and etiquette, 78–79

and nonverbal behavior, 69–72
and not putting yourself down,
  75–76
and preparation, 79–80
and smiling, 73–75
and taking compliments, 76–77
cleaning lady, hiring a, 149–150
Clinton, Bill, 31, 73, 166
Clinton, Hillary Rodham, 48, 165, 193
coaches, professional, 122–124
collaboration, 99
college degree, 132
communication, 42–64
  assertiveness in, 60–61
  avoiding "but" syndrome in, 52–53
  business vs. personal, 50–52
  and conversation, 46–47
  depersonalization of, 45
  and getting to the point, 55–57
  and giggling, 61–62
  indirect vs. direct style of, 57–60
  and interrupting, 53–55
  and networking, 141
  and overcoming gender bias, 47–50
  and saying that you're sorry, 62–63
  styles of, 43–46
competition, thriving on, 137–139
complacency, avoiding, 111–113
compliments, taking, 76–77
computers, 82, 127
confrontation, 93–96
conversation, 46–47
Cosby, Bill, on key to failure, 92
Creating Women's Networks, 20–21
creativity and creative thinking,
  135–137
crying, 98
cultures, organizational, 18–20

Dain Rauscher, 20
Danforth, Jack, 171
Daniels, Carol, 53–54
decision-making styles, 54–55
Decker, Wayne, on humor, 74
Delay, Tom, 94–95
delegation, 146–149
Deutsche Bank, 27
directness, rudeness vs., 60
divorce, as threat to financial security,
  176–177
documentation of sexual harassment,
  38

Dole, Bob, 166
Dole, Elizabeth, 17, 170–171
domestic violence, 35
Dorf, Heather
  on competitiveness, 138
  on learning from mentors, 57
downsizing, 82
Dressel, Barbara
  on being feminine, 60
  on communicating, 44–45
  on delegation, 146
  on getting respect, 92–93
  on insecure women, 124
  on success, 155
  on walking away from things, 152
Drucker, Peter
  on hierarchies, 86
  on leaders of nonprofit organiza-
    tions, 29
Dubois, Ellen Carol, 164
Duell, Charles, 135
dynamic leadership, 86–88

e-commerce, 128–131
Edlhuber, Deb, 128–129
education, 131–133
Edward Jones, 20
EEOC, see U.S. Equal Employment
    Opportunity Commission
elder care, 192–193
Elman, Carolyn, 39, 87, 194
  on feeling emotional, 98
  on mentor training, 120
  on women in mixed groups, 142
Emerson, Ralph Waldo, on good
    manners, 78
emotional control, 96–98
employee manual, 37
employees, problem, 88–90
entrepreneurs, 9
entrepreneurs, women, 30–32, 128,
    157–158
Equal Employment Opportunity
    Commission, 8
Equal Pay Act, 8
etiquette, 78–79
executives, wage gap among, 9
executive summaries, 56
exercise, 157
expectations, 3–10
  and attitudes about gender inequity,
    4–10

of success, 3–4, 9–10
eye contact, 73

failure, 109, 110
family, work and, 189–197
  and being a role model, 193–197
  and sex roles, 190–191
  and shared responsibility, 191–193
Feit, Ronnie, 174
"feminine charm," using, 84–86
The Feminine Mystique (Betty
    Friedan), 191
Feminist Majority Foundation, 7
fidgeting, 71
financial security, 174–187
  and asking for what you're worth,
    180–182
  benefits of, 183
  divorce as threat to, 176–177
  and economic necessity, 183–184
  getting help in achieving, 184–186
  and paying yourself first, 186–187
  responsibility for, 177–178
  and wage gap, 178–180
  widowhood as threat to, 175–176
Finestone, Laura
  on coaching, 123–124
  on competition with women, 125
  on nurturing yourself, 151–152
Fiorina, Carly, 26
Firestone, Marsha
  on being a role model for children,
    195
  on future for women, 198
  on nonverbal communication,
    69–71
  on tilting your head, 72
Fisher, Helen, 198
focus days, 161–162
Forbes magazine, 189–190
Ford, Henry, on thinking you can or
    can't, 1
Ford Motor Company, 34
Fortune magazine, 6, 74, 118, 125
Franklin, Benjamin, on value of
    education, 131–133
Fraser, Edie, 118, 192
  on continuing education, 132
  on technology and competitiveness,
    129
  on women in politics, 170
Freud, Sigmund, 71

Freytag, Vanessa
  on accepting a new job, 115
  on changing workforce, 191
  on future for women, 198
  on getting all the information,
    55–56
  on leadership, 87
  on management style, 83
  on negotiation, 99
  on open-door policies, 91
  on reducing stress, 156–157
  on taking compliments, 77
  on trusting your instincts, 150–151
Friedan, Betty, 191
future, the, 197–199

gender bias
  insidiousness of, 25
  overcoming, 47–50
gender differences, 21–22, 43–45
General Electric (GE), 8
geographic differences, 29–30
Getting to Yes, 99
giggling, 61–62
Gilberd, Pamela, 198
Gilman, Barb
  on humor, 75
  on money, 183
  on refusing to fail, 109–111
glass ceiling, *xii*, 19, 24–30
Glatzer, Bonnie, 25–26
  on complaint procedures, 37
  on crying, 98
  on delegation, 147
  on finding male allies, 39
  on mentors, 117–118
  on negotiation, 100
  on self-deprecation, 75–76
  on speaking up, 121
  on taking time for yourself, 157
goals, reaching your, *see* long-term
  goals, reaching
Gold, Christina, 18–19
Goodall, Jane, 72
good ole boys' network, 139
Gore, Al, 128, 195
Gray, John, 43–44, 129–130
gray-matter glass ceiling, 25
Grelck, Mona, on working in a
  traditional male industry, 57
Grode, Susan, 120
gut feelings, trusting your, 150–151

Hadary, Sharon, 22, 31
  on collaboration, 99
  on decision-making styles, 54–55
  on having credibility, 132
  on letting others know about your
    success, 105
  on participating in conversation, 54
  on taking compliments, 77
  on white male and other models, 21
Hagberg, Richard, 82–83
Hagberg Consulting Group, 82–83
Harriman, Karen, 35, 195
  on being a bitch, 93
  on being angry, 97–98
  on direct communication, 60–61
  on directness vs. rudeness, 60
  on maintaining your true essence,
    152
  on nonprofit organizations, 29
  on success, 154
  on taking time for herself, 157
head
  nodding your, 71–72
  tilting your, 72
headhunters, 182
Hedrick, Darla, on being assertive, 53
Helgesen, Sally, 83
Henry, Sherrye, 31, 33, 167
Hewlett Packard, 26
Hierarchy of Needs, 87–88
Hill, Anita, 33
Hudanich, Sarah
  on being your own career manager,
    102
  on her role model, 16
  on making decisions, 159
  on saying you're sorry, 63
  on success, 154–155
  on trusting your instincts, 150
  on women as leaders, 88–89, 91
humor, 74–75
Hwang, Mary, on SCORE, 59

IBM Corporation, 16, 88–89
inclusive, being, 142–143
internal networking programs, 20
Internet, 128–131, 185
interrupting, 53–55
intimacy, in communication, 50–52
investing, 185–186
invitation, waiting for an, 13–14
Ireland, Patricia, 167–168, 197

ITT Commercial Finance, 27

Jacobsen, Linda
    on delegation, 148
    on eye contact, 73
    on gender communications, 44
    on taking risks, 108
    on "threatened women," 126
Jordan, Barbara, on politics, 163
Jung, Andrea, 19

Keats, John, on failure, 110
Keller, Helen, 199
Kim, Angie, on e-commerce, 129

Landrieu, Mary, 47
lateral transfers, 113–116
Lauren, Ralph, on leaders, 81
Lazarus, Shelly, 153
leadership, 81–100
    and avoiding the "disease to please,"
        92–93
    and confrontation, 93–96
    and disciplining/terminating
        problem employees, 88–90
    dynamic, 86–88
    and emotional control, 96–98
    and negotiation, 98–100
    and the new economy, 81–84
    and open-door policies, 90–92
    and use of feminine charm, 84–86
League of Women Voters, 172
learning
    from others, 17–18
    by reading, 133–134
long-term goals, reaching, 102–116
    and avoiding complacency, 111–113
    and creating awareness in others,
        105–106
    with lateral/interindustry moves,
        113–116
    mission statement for, 103
    and positive attitude, 110–111
    and taking risks, 107–110
    by "wowing" others, 104–107
Los Angeles Times, 27

MacLachlan, Mary Lehman, 177, 179,
    184–185, 187, 196
Malcolm, Ellen, 166
male bashing, 44–45
manual, employee, 37

marriage, 177
Martin, Christy, 182
Martin, Lynn, on glass ceiling, 24
Martin, Whitney Johns, on communi-
    cation differences between men
    and women, 43
Maslow, Abraham, 87–88
Massachusetts Institute of Technology
    (MIT), 28
McBeal, Ally, 69
McEntire, Margaret, 108–109
McNair, Ronald E., on walking over
    the edge, 107
Mead, Margaret, on mother's role, 190
media, 47–48
*Men Are from Mars, Women Are from
    Venus* (John Gray), 43–44
mentors, 57, 117–122
Milken Institute, 32
mission statement, 103
MIT (Massachusetts Institute of
    Technology), 28
Mitsubishi, 34
money
    borrowing, 43
    thinking about, 185
    see also financial security
Morley, Christopher, on success, 153
Mosbacher, Georgette, on politics as
    man's game, 170
mytop theory, 146

National Association of Women
    Business Owners (NAWBO), 165
National Committee on Pay Equity, 8
National Foundation for Women
    Business Owners (NFWBO), 9,
    30, 54, 128
National Women's Business Council,
    32
NAWBO, *see* National Association of
    Women Business Owners
Neese, Terry, 167, 169, 171–172
negotiation
    and leadership, 98–100
    and wage gap, 179–180
networking, 103, 139–142
networking programs, internal, 20
new economy, 81–84, 135
Newsweek magazine, 24–25
Newton, Catherine Garda, 36
    on competition, 138

Newton, Catherine Garda (*continued*)
  on confrontation styles, 95
  on doing what you like, 153
  on dressing like a woman, 68
  on emotional control, 97
  on learning from managers, 17
  on letting others know about your
    success, 105–106
  on success, 155
  on taking executive positions, 115
  on walking into a room, 71
NFWBO, *see* National Foundation for
  Women Business Owners
Nineteenth Amendment, 163
no, saying, 159–160
nodding your head, 71–72
nonassertive communication style,
  57–59
nonprofit organizations, 29
nonverbal communication, 69–72

Office of Advocacy (Small Business
  Administration), 9
Office of Women's Procurement, 32
open-door policies, 90–92
opportunities, creating your own,
  12–14
organizational cultures, 18–20

pampering yourself, 155–159
The Paper Warehouse, 12
passion, following your, 151–153
paying yourself first, 186–187
perfectionism, 147
permission, waiting for, 11–12
personal appearance, 67–69
personal bio, creating a, 107
personal chitchat, 52
P&L experience, 27
political correctness, 26
politics, 163–173
  funding for women in, 170–172
  getting involved in, 168–169
  need for diversity in, 167–168
  training for women to become
    active in, 172–173
  underrepresentation of women in,
    164–167
  and women's suffrage movement,
    163–164
positive, being, 77–78, 110–111
power, *xii–xiii*

Power Etiquette (Dana May
  Casperson), 79
praising, giving, 106
preparation, importance of, 79–80
Pretty Woman, 70
problem employees, disciplining/ter-
  minating, 88–90
Proctor and Gamble, 19–20
professional coaches, 122–124
professionalism, and preparation,
  79–80
Professional Women of Southwestern
  Bell (PWSB), 19
profit-and-loss (P&L) experience, 27
putting yourself down, 75–76
PWSB (Professional Women of
  Southwestern Bell), 19

reading, learning by, 133–134
reengineering, 82
Reno, Janet, 17
resignations, 5
retaliation, for sexual harassment
  complaints, 37–38
Rimm, Sylvia, 137
risks, taking, 107–110
Roath, Nancy, 130–131
Roberts, Flori
  on being a role model for girls, 196
  on CEOs, 86–87
  on developing a personal look,
    68–69
  on humor, 74–75
  on investing, 184
  on personal appearance, 71
  on prioritizing, 159–160
  on sharing control, 147
  on women as leaders, 83, 88
Rogers, Adrian, 25
role model
  being a, 193–197
  finding a, 16–17
Ross, Ann, 11–12, 89–90
rudeness, directness vs., 60
Russell, Elizabeth, 30

Salsman, Iris, 111–112
  on doing what you like, 153
  on financial control, 183
  on humor, 74
  on playing to the audience, 46
  on talking about money, 180–181

SBA, *see* U.S. Small Business
    Administration
Schroeder, Pat, 170
SCORE (Service Corps of Retired
    Executives), 59
Scott, Jan, 28
Scribner, Susan
    on etiquette, 78–79
    on personal appearance, 67
See Jane Win (Sylvia Rimm), 137
Segal, Eric
    on advantages of female leader
        ship, 18
    on career moves, 114, 115
    on career planning, 103
    on getting a degree, 133
    on getting out of dead-end
        positions, 113
    on headhunters, 182
    on increased opportunities for
        women, 18
    on wage gap, 179, 180
self-actualization, 87–88
self-deprecation, 75–76
Serlin, Marsha, 36
    on being feminine, 85
    on being too tolerant, 90
    on getting paid, 95
    on good ole boys, 140
    on handling telephone requests,
        160
    on mentoring, 119–120
    on need to interrupt, 54
    on parenting responsibilities, 192
    on taking risks, 109
    on taking things personally, 92
    on taking time for yourself, 158
    on "threatened women," 126
Service Corps of Retired Executives
    (SCORE), 59
sex roles, 190–191
sexual discrimination, 24, 26–32
    see also glass ceiling
sexual harassment, 32–39
    and documentation, 38
    emotional/financial costs of, 33–34
    and finding male allies, 38–39
    and knowing your rights, 35–36
    lawsuits/settlements involving, 34
    prevalence of, 32–33
    skepticism about claims of, 34
    taking steps to combat, 36–38

Sherberg, Ellen, on great vs. near
    great, 109
signature look, creating a, 67–69
Simmons, Stephanie
    on creating a support team, 149
    on focus days, 161–162
Simons, Jill, on direct communication,
    61
Small Business Administration, 9
Smeal, Eleanor, on leading the way,
    189
smiling, 73–75
societal attitudes, 2–10
Society for Human Resource
    Management, 27
Solovic, Susan, on money, 183
sorry, saying you're, 62–63
The Sound of Music, 111
Southern Baptist Convention, 25
Southwestern Bell, 19, 134
speaking up, 49, 120–122
special connection, creating a, 72–73
Spectrum, 57
Spiegal, Shelly, 133
spirituality, 158–159
sports, talking about, 47
Stanton, Elizabeth Cady, 164, 178–
    179
Steinem, Gloria, 12
stress, 155–159
success, defining your, 153–155
Suhocki, Bobbe, 20, 150
superwoman complex, 145–146
Supreme Court, 8
Swiss, Deborah, 85

Tannen, Deborah, 51, 62
team, building a supportive, 14–15,
    149
technology, as gender equalizer,
    127–131
Tennyson, Alfred Lord, on women,
    124
Ternes, Patricia, 20
Texaco, 179
"threatened woman," 124–127
Thurmond, Strom, 47
time management, 160–162
"to do" lists, 161
trade journals, writing for, 106–107
training, political, 172–173
"troubles talk," 51–52

Turner, Ellen, 114

United States Supreme Court, 17
U.S. Equal Employment Opportunity
    Commission (EEOC), 34, 37
U.S. Small Business Administration
    (SBA), 31, 32

Vandiver, Donna, on being ignored,
    48–49
voice tonality and inflections, 49–50

wage gap, 7–9, 178–180
waiting
    for an invitation, 13
    for permission, 11–12
    walking into a room, 70, 71
Wall Street Journal, 5
Washington University, 28
Wayne, Claudia, 34–35
    on divorce laws, 177
    on need to negotiate, 180
    on wage gap, 8–9
Weaver, Juanita
    on networking, 139–142
    on speed in new economy, 135
Welch, Jack, 87
Wellington, Sheila, 19
Westinghouse, 8
The White House Project, 168

white male model, 21
Wicks, Vicki, on negative people, 15
widowhood, as threat to financial
    security, 175–176
Wilkinson, Barbara, 19
    on executive summaries, 56
    on leaders, 148
    on learning, 134
    on learning from successful people,
        17
    on mentoring, 119
    on women's groups, 19, 143
    on working with others, 93
Wilson, Marie, 168
Winfrey, Oprah, 17
"winging it," 79–80
Women Breaking Through (Deborah
    Swiss), 85
women-owned businesses, 9
women's suffrage movement,
    163–164
Wood, Kathy, 160–161
Woods, Harriet, 11, 165–166, 168–169,
    171
Working Girl, 133
"wowing" others, 104–107
Wyse, Lois, on apologizing by men
    and women, 75

Zeilmann, Judy, 13–14